Political Participation in a Changing World

T0347642

In the last decades, political participation has expanded continuously. This expansion includes activities as diverse as voting, tweeting, signing petitions, changing your social media profile, demonstrating, boycotting products, joining flash mobs, attending meetings, throwing seedbombs, and donating money. But if political participation is so diverse, how do we recognize participation when we see it? Despite the growing interest in new forms of citizen engagement in politics, there is virtually no systematic research investigating what these new and emerging forms of engagement look like, how prevalent they are in various societies, and how they fit within the broader structure of well-known participatory acts conceptually and empirically. The rapid spread of internet-based activities especially underlines the urgency to deal with such challenges.

In this book, Yannis Theocharis and Jan W. van Deth put forward a systematic and unified approach to explore political participation and offer new conceptual and empirical tools with which to study it. *Political Participation in a Changing World* will assist both scholars and students of political behavior to systematically study new forms of political participation without losing track of more conventional political activities.

Yannis Theocharis is Research Fellow at the Mannheim Centre for European Social Research (MZES), University of Mannheim, Germany. His research focuses on political behavior, political communication, new media, and social networks. He was an Alexander von Humboldt Fellow and has co-directed several projects investigating the impact of social media on politics. His work has appeared in political science and communication journals such as *Journal of Communication, European Political Science Review, New Media & Society*, and *Electoral Studies*.

Jan W. van Deth is Professor Emeritus of Political Science and International Comparative Social Research at the University of Mannheim, Germany. His research areas are political culture (especially social capital, political engagement, and citizenship), social change, and comparative research methods. He is a Corresponding Member of the Royal Netherlands Academy of Arts and Sciences (KNAW) and Project Director at the MZES. His publications appeared in leading international journals and with high-ranked publishers.

"Citizen political participation is increasing and diversifying in contemporary democracies. *Political Participation in a Changing World* provides a theoretical guide to this rich and expanding literature. Theocharis and van Deth present a valuable summary of the research evidence and the new research questions in the participation field."

—*Russell J. Dalton, University of California*

"*Political Participating in a Changing World* addresses several scholarly debates associated with studying how, where, and why citizens engage in politics. The authors argue that participation research has not sufficiently acknowledged societal developments such as globalization, digitalization, and individualization. Theocharis and van Deth attempt to remedy this weakness by identifying five distinct modes of participation that can be used to study how and why citizens engage in and beyond the parliamentary realm of politics. This book offers important advice about studying participation in looser and transnational governance settings that use citizen action to address complex, borderless problems."

—*Michele Micheletti, Stockholm University*

Political Participation in a Changing World

Conceptual and Empirical Challenges in the Study of Citizen Engagement

Yannis Theocharis
and Jan W. van Deth

LONDON AND NEW YORK

First published 2018 by Routledge

2 Park Square, Milton Park, Abingdon, Oxfordshire OX14 4RN
52 Vanderbilt Avenue, New York, NY 10017

Routledge is an imprint of the Taylor & Francis Group, an informa business

First issued in paperback 2019

Library of Congress Cataloging-in-Publication Data
A catalog record for this book has been requested

ISBN: 978-1-138-30598-4 (hbk)
ISBN: 978-0-367-89140-4 (pbk)

Typeset in Sabon
by Apex CoVantage, LLC

This book is dedicated to Popi, Rigas, and Joke

Contents

Figures

Tables

Preface

Whereas many pundits warn about the permanent "crises" of democracy, the continuous rise of new ways of citizen engagement seems to tell a different story. Today, the list of available means to express social and political opinions and to influence decision-making procedures is virtually endless and includes such diverse activities as casting a vote, writing a blog, demonstrating, or buying a specific brand of coffee and encouraging others on Twitter to do the same. This amazing expansion of the repertoire of political participation in many democracies presents many challenges for theory-guided empirical research. How to avoid the case that constantly emerging new modes of political participation are simply neglected by dated conceptualizations? How to include principally non-political activities in the study of participation without stretching concepts and instruments to cover everything? And do internet-based activities revolutionize the repertoire of political participation?

The idea for this book was born in September 2015 at the annual meeting of the American Political Science Association in sunny San Francisco. Whereas the conference program included numerous contributions and many panels about all things participation, a common underlying pattern in the presentations was a lack of a common understanding about what constitutes political participation. Also common was that scholars working on young people's political (dis)engagement, digital politics, and extra-institutionalized participation, employed wildly different ways to operationalize and measure participation beyond the electoral arena. In short, despite the general agreement among both senior and junior scholars that the world is changing rapidly and something "new" is happening that needs to be captured empirically and studied thoroughly, no common language seemed to exist that could tie together the diverse concepts and methods for studying and analyzing the constantly expanding repertoire of participation. This state of affairs was very much in line with the theme of the conference, which was "diversities reconsidered"; as the organizers put it, "we seek to reconsider and reflect on these various diversities [. . .] how do we define, conceptualize, and include diversities in the issues we address and the methods we employ". These very same diversities in the study of political participation resulted, of course, in much discussion and disagreement among scholars as to what exactly they were measuring, how much of it was out there, and what was its value for democracy.

The San Francisco experiences confirmed our impression that a unified conceptual framework is missing from the study of participation—a common vocabulary that would allow for a more systematic and comparative empirical study of the ways in which citizens engage politically, and for more fruitful exchanges between scholars working in this area. Encouraged by the critical reception of our previous work on the topic, we decided to integrate, build on, and considerably expand the arguments that we have developed in our research on new forms of political participation in the last few years. The aim of this book is to explore the main limitations in studying political participation today, and to propose a new approach that allows to study this very important topic systematically—both conceptually and empirically—in a rapidly changing world.

The Mannheim Centre for European Social Research (MZES) at the University of Mannheim (Germany) provided an ideal base for our ramble through the minefields of advanced comparative and behavioral research. Besides, the PartiRep-II project of the Belgian Science Policy Office (Belspo) provided us with funding for a conference on the study of new forms of participation in September 2014, and for the collection of new data to explore the potential gains of our approach. We would like to express our gratitude for these unbureaucratic and very helpful backings over a long period of time.

This book could not have been written without the willingness of many people to stimulate and defy our ideas in usually rather long discussions and in extensive comments on drafts of our papers. We especially would like to thank Gema García-Albacete, Rüdiger Schmitt-Beck, and Kateřina Vráblíková for their patience and very valuable and detailed comments on earlier parts of the arguments presented here. Very helpful comments were also provided in discussions on this or closely related topics with Lance Bennet, Shelley Boulianne, Rachel Gibson, Marc Hooghe, Bengü Hosch-Dayican, Andreas Jungherr, Tom van der Meer, Joost de Moor, Sebastian Popa, Ellen Quintelier, Christian Schnaudt, Carole Uhlaner, Michael Xenos, Sonja Zmerli, and

Carolin Zorell. Yannis Theocharis is also grateful to the members of the Social Media and Political Participation (SMaPP) lab at New York University who provided an excellent forum for discussing many of the conceptual and empirical issues in the study of digitally networked participation several times. We are very grateful to be surrounded by colleagues who always showed their expertise by criticizing our ideas without reluctance, and their friendship and generosity by always suggesting thought-provoking rival interpretations and possible solutions.

Yannis Theocharis and Jan W. van Deth
Mannheim, June 2017

1 Would You Recognize a Form of Political Participation if You Saw One?

> The mass of citizens play a passive, quiescent, even apathetic part, responding only to the signals given them.
>
> (Crouch 2004, 4)

1.1 The Many Faces of Participation

On a warm, sunny day in California in 2014, wearing only a pair of jeans and grinning expectantly and uncontrollably towards the camera, John was preparing to have a bucketful of cold water with a generous amount of ice cubes emptied on his head. He had been nominated by Jane—who can be seen standing behind him struggling to lift the heavy bucket—for the "ALS ice-bucket challenge". It will remain a mystery to those of us who don't know John (but who, along with eleven million others, saw the tagged YouTube video) whether the three seconds that followed (during which Jane, after losing control of the bucket and dumping it with its contents on John's head, slipped herself on the fallen ice cubes leading to hysterical laughs from everybody present) made him regret his decision to promote awareness of the amyotrophic lateral sclerosis disease (ALS) in this fashion. One thing is certain: With $220 million raised by millions of videos tagged for the 2014 and 2015 challenge, coverage by the *New York Times*, the *Guardian* and other popular daily newspapers and media outlets, and videos posted from such people as Barack Obama and George W. Bush, to Lady Gaga and Rihanna, the steering committee of the ALS association was delighted with John's engagement in their campaign.

At around the same time in Austria, students of the Technical University of Vienna were engaged in a very different campaign over a figure that could probably have allowed the ALS association to fund research on the disease for the next millennium: 19 billion euros—an amount of money sufficient enough to build an entire new city. The students erected "Hypotopia", a model city of more than 1,200 components over four months at Vienna's Karlsplatz (one of the city's main squares). Had it been actually built, this new city would have been the sixth largest in Austria. The plan, students argued, could have materialized using the money that the Austrian government used to bail out the failed Hypo Alpe Adria bank. The aim of the students, who started the endeavor after being disappointed that a petition calling for an official enquiry didn't gather enough signatures, was to visualize the scale of the bailout for the general public. With meticulous attention to detail (the city was created according to industrial standards and planning included everything from the costs of soil excavations and education to rubbish incinerators), the project became, in one of the project's founders' words "more than just an architecture project, it's a protest in concrete" (The Guardian 2014).

Residents of Vienna passing through Karlsplatz may have realized in shock what could be done with 19 billion euros. It was also a shock for global public opinion to slowly discover through reports on Twitter and photos on Instagram the magnitude of the riots in Ferguson, Missouri, in 2014. These uprisings were a direct reaction to the shooting of Michael Brown, a black citizen, and to police violence and race discrimination. Armed with smartphones and the courage needed to enter the burning and embattled zone, thousands of people took and tagged photos and tweets with hashtags such as #Dontshoot and #Ferguson, creating online content that could no longer be ignored by mainstream media (The Atlantic 2015). Four months later, following the news that a grand jury would not indict the policeman who shot Brown, protests erupted once again in the city and the hashtags #Dontshoot and #BlackLivesMatter were used for raising awareness of the injustice. On 10 December 2014, in a witty self-expressive fashion, Harvard students joined by faculty staged a "die-in" for 15½ minutes to protest Michael Brown's death along with that of Eric Garner, a black man killed in New York by the police (The Boston Globe 2014).

Somewhat later, John Doe in Houston, Texas, was watching quietly on his sofa how the Republican presidential nominee Donald J. Trump announced his plan to deport 11 million undocumented immigrants. John, a staunch Republican, hadn't missed an election since he became eligible to vote a long time ago. Although he wasn't sure about this bombastic candidate, he was already planning to attend the local party meeting that afternoon (even though the fact that attendance of such party meetings had kept waning over the last years, which made them less exciting than a few decades ago). His wife Tara, a frequent volunteer at Keegan Kitchen, a Houston-based organization that prepares meals for hungry kids, was sitting at the other end reading with some amusement on her tablet that the ALS association was planning to establish the ice-bucket challenge as an annual event. The couple was expecting their younger daughter, Sally, and her partner, Marcus, for dinner. This would be their last dinner together for at least a month, as Sally and Marcus were feverishly preparing for their trip to Paris. Marcus was a delegate of a well-known organization in the forthcoming "United Nations Climate Change Conference", as well as one of the organizers of the organization's direct actions including demonstrations, street theater performances, flash mobs, and the handing over of thousands of petitions—enough reasons to prompt (yet again) heated discussions at the Does' dinner table.[1]

Diseases, the financial crisis, race discrimination, police violence, presidential campaigns, immigration, and global warming are only some of the topics that pop up frequently. Citizens are concerned about these matters and want to defend their interests, influence the behavior of authorities, look for like-minded others, or simply express their opinions in a public manner. For these purposes, a large number of actions and activities are available: Casting a vote, demonstrating, blogging, attacking police blockades, working for a candidate, attending a rally, writing a tweet to encourage others to support a campaign, signing a petition, boycotting products, supporting PACs, signing up on a campaign website, and donating money are well-known specimens. Although these activities all take place within the broader locus of what people today understand as politics, it is less clear whether they constitute acts of *political* participation. In their seminal work *Participation in America*, Sidney Verba and Norman Nie defined political participation as "those activities by private citizens that are more or less directly aimed at influencing the selection of governmental personnel and/or the actions they take" (1972, 2). The authors themselves immediately admit that, although this definition is rough, it is adequate for delimiting their sphere of interest as acts aimed at influencing governmental decisions. Whereas few scholars would dispute that attending a party meeting or participating in a demonstration constitute acts of political participation, the same characterization will inevitably raise a few eyebrows when referring to designing a model city or to tweeting an image with your hands raised and tagging it with #Dontshoot. As these last mentioned acts usually are not even aimed at "influencing the selection of governmental personnel and/or the actions they take", in much academic scholarship they simply are not covered by concepts of political participation. Does this matter for our understanding of political participation?

The simple depiction of all kind of activities as political participation without dealing with the conceptual and empirical aspects involved is troubling. That participation has expanded well beyond electoral and party politics is, of course, old news. Many scholars have theorized and empirically documented this expansion outside the electoral arena impressively (Norris 2002; Barnes et al. 1979; Stolle, Hooghe, and Micheletti 2005; Micheletti and McFarland 2010; Inglehart 1990). Participation has expanded rapidly into extra-institutional domains and is expressed in a large number of lifestyle- and internet-based modes of engagement that, in principle, can be pursued by each individual citizen. Some such activities can be seen as modes of "individualized collective action" (Micheletti 2003, 24–30) that do not require collective or organized action, and increasingly include "non-political activities used for political purposes" (van Deth 2014, 358). By now almost every conceivable non-private activity by some citizen can be sometimes understood as a form of political participation (van Deth 2001; van Deth 2015), be it the tipping of ice-buckets, the design of a new city, the selection of a presidential candidate, or blocking streets in Paris.

This book deals with the continuous expansion—and fragmentation—of the repertoire of political participation and puts forward a systematic unified vision of the concept of political participation. Its major aim is to offer a conceptual and empirical fairway to sail between the *Charybdis* of excluding many new modes of political participation by using dated conceptualizations, and the *Scylla* of stretching concepts and instruments to cover almost everything. Crucial questions, therefore, to be dealt with in this book are these:

1. Given the difficulty of detecting political acts that may not fit squarely within available definitions of participation, how do we recognize political participation if we see it?
2. In light of the expansion and use of non-political activities for political purposes, how do we avoid falling into the trap of considering everything as political participation?
3. (a) How can new forms of political participation be measured? And do they fit into a general taxonomy of participatory activities?
   (b) How widespread are new forms of political participation and who uses them?
4. How can our approach and findings be used by researchers who want to study new and emerging forms of political participation but do not want to exclude more conventional forms?

1.2 The Argument of the Book

The continuous rise of new forms of engaging with political and social affairs—an expansion that often includes acts of extremely minimal, or no, costs—and the gradual decline in institutionalized participation, has been a cause for concern to both scholars and pundits (Schlozman, Verba, and Brady 2012; Milner 2010; Morozov 2009). Can activities such as blogging or posting photos on Instagram in support of the Black Lives Mater (BLM) movement be considered as specimens of political participation—that is, as activities that basically belong to the same category as voting or contacting a politician? Austrian students told the *Guardian* that they "felt the creation of Hypotopia had a strong impact on public perception of the scandal" and that their project gave a "signal to politicians that this will go on further". Engagement by thousands on social media not only elevated the Ferguson riots and the issue of racial discrimination to the top of the local and national agenda (CBS News 2014), but, according to the *Washington Post*, played a major role in documenting conditions on the ground, organizing protesters and building awareness and literacy (Washington Post 2014). Apparently, even although such activities would not fit Verba and Nie's classic definition of political participation cited in the last section (p. 3), people involved in these kinds of activities want to attract public attention for some cause and, consequently, influence decision-making processes just as voters do. Yet it is clear that these city designers and anti-racism twitterers are more eagerly looking for opportunities to express their opinions and to make moral statements in public, than to reach specific goals or to wait four years till the next election. The spread of new forms of participation seems to be especially related to this change in priorities among citizens.

Changing priorities among citizens can be seen through the lens of modernization theory. Modernization literature argues that a process of intergenerational value change has been transforming citizens' values for quite some time. This process has reduced allegiances to the state and respect for authorities while, at the same time, has brought new political issues to the forefront and new ways to advocate them (Inglehart 2007; Welzel 2013; Dalton and Welzel 2014; Inglehart 1977). As a result, citizens' conceptions and norms of what it means to be a "good" citizen are moving away from the dutiful and obedient, allegiant to the state, paradigm (Schudson 1998) that is inextricably linked to voting as the hallmark of political participation, and party membership as the main avenue for being represented (Dalton, Scarrow, and Cain 2004; Dalton and Wattenberg 2000). Furthermore, the scope of government activities and responsibilities expanded in many countries, resulting in a considerable growth of the domain of political participation; that is, political participation became relevant in areas that would be considered private, social, or economic only recently (van Deth 2001). With the popularization of the internet in the late 1990s and the rise and widespread use of new information and communication technologies (such as smartphones) and Web 2.0 platforms (like social media) in the mid- and late-2000s, communication and mobilization for political activities have also become very easy.

Among citizens, the effects of these societal and technological changes are reflected in the blurring of the distinction between private and public spheres, the rise in skills and resources (especially education), and the availability of an abundance of political information, incentives, and opportunities for participation. These developments are accompanied by declines in voter turnout across advanced democracies, a drop in civic engagement, and a massive deterioration of party membership as one of the major institutions of representative democracy (Putnam 2000; Wattenberg 2002; Dalton and Wattenberg 2000; Norris 2002). There is less participation in politics through institutionalized avenues, and more participation through extra-institutionalized, personalized, self-expressive, and individualized forms. For instance, the group Bite the Ballot (2017), a strictly apartisan local lunch-time club turned into a national youth-led movement and identified by the *Guardian* as rejecting the entire political system, defines itself as "solution-focused citizens", "individuals with unique identities", and "issued-based participants" with the mission to "empower young citizens to lead change that they want to see in society". These "Everyday Makers", as Bang (2005) has called them, may still vote and keep themselves informed about politics, but they refuse to acquire their political identities from being citizens of the state, or members of an interest group or a social movement. Research has shown that they are rather concerned to enhance their personal capacities for self-governance and co-governance (Li and Marsh 2008). Moreover, as Harris, Wyn, and Younes (2010) note, despite being disenchanted with political structures which they feel are unresponsive to their needs and interests, they remain interested in social and political issues and continue to seek recognition from the political system. The rationale, therefore, guiding many of the participatory behaviors that we are witnessing today, may be the outcome of a number of different considerations associated with having your voice heard while at the same time making the most out of your everyday experience in a "do it yourself", "do it where you are", "do it for fun, but also because you find it necessary", or "do it with the system, if need be" fashion (Bang 2005, 169). In short, political participation is not vanishing; the repertoire of available forms is expanding continuously, rapidly, and beyond what we have traditionally understood as being part of politically active citizenship.

In light of these developments, we argue that the expansion of political participation presents three major challenges: a theoretical, a conceptual, and a methodological/empirical one.

1.2.1 Political Participation Expanded: Theoretical Issues

Many of the new forms of political participation hardly resemble what we usually perceive as political participation. Mixing clay soil, compost, and seeds with water in order to make a "seedbomb" (which later on can be dropped at an area in your neighborhood that has been ravaged by concrete), is not, by any order of magnitude, an activity "by private citizens [. . .] more or less directly aimed at influencing the selection of governmental personnel and/or the actions they take" (Verba and Nie 1972, 2). Nor is using a hashtag on Twitter or Facebook in order to raise awareness for an anti-racism campaign among your social circle. Contrary to the position taken by Verba and Nie—who were adamant that *democratic* participation should, above all, refer to "the actual behavior of citizens in attempting to influence the government" (Verba and Nie 1972, 3)—these forms are not aimed at government officials and they do not even take place within the locus of government. The important point here is that, if these forms of participation are not defined as political, it is hard to see why one should assign them any democratic relevance at all. On the other hand, many of these activities are not only perceived as politically meaningful by some citizens, but they are the main way in which these people engage with politics—or, as some have argued, they are the reason that brings them into more formal participatory arenas such as civic and political organizations (Penney 2015).

The direct outcome of this state of affairs is that, although the level of political participation may appear low to those who define participation in the traditional sense, it may, at the same time, appear high to those who are prone to adopting a more open definition. The *theoretical* problem created by this contradictory perception of what it means to participate in democratic politics is a major one. Why?

A very large amount of political behavior research over the last two decades has been concerned with the decline of civic and political participation (Wattenberg 2002; Fieldhouse, Tranmer, and Russell 2007;

Marsh, O'Toole, and Jones 2007; Pharr and Putnam 2000; Franklin 2004; Hay 2007; Stoker 2006; Blais, Gidengil, and Nevitte 2004; Torcal and Montero 2006; Putnam 2000; Wattenberg 2002; Dalton and Wattenberg 2000). Many of those scholars warned explicitly for the disconcerting effects of this development for the health of democracy (Torcal and Montero 2006; Kaase and Newton 1995; Putnam 2000). Yet, more often than not, this research has treated political participation as synonymous to institutionalized participation that occurs within the electoral arena (for an extensive discussion see Norris 2002), or with protest activities directly aimed at decision-making processes in that arena (Barnes et al. 1979). This is partly due to the ways in which participation has been defined and measured over the last decades (see the next two subsections), and partly because institutionalized acts, such as voting or standing for office, have traditionally been considered as the cornerstones of democratic engagement (Lazarsfeld, Berelson, and Gaudet 1948; Downs 1957; Verba and Nie 1972; Berelson, Lazarsfeld, and McPhee 1954)—an idea few would disagree with.

As Verba and Nie perceptively remarked more than 40 years ago, "the more narrowly one limits the scope of what one considers participation, the smaller the amount one will find" (Verba and Nie 1972, 29). From a theoretical standpoint, therefore, scholars relying on an institutionally focused approach will not recognize newer forms of participation as politically and democratically meaningful and, consequently, will tend to assess political participation as being in decline (and probably that democracy is in danger). Those who use broader approaches will stress the continuous expansion of available forms of participation (and probably provide a more positive assessment of democracy). Debates about the extent of political disengagement and the health of democracy are often characterized by such misapprehensions (Norris 1999; Dalton 2008; Putnam 2000) and look like discussions between deaf people, each of them—correctly—claiming to have the best arguments.

1.2.2 *Political Participation Expanded: Conceptual Issues*

The advantages of sticking to an established concept of political participation such as the cited definition of Verba and Nie are evident. First, connections to the existing literature are unproblematic and accumulation of knowledge and collaborative work are espoused. Second, the crucial links of a concept to theoretical notions and their empirical measures are comprehensible. These advantages have to be weighed against the gains of redefining or expanding a concept. In the case of political participation these gains are clear: Assessing whether democracy is at risk due to depleting and/or expanding levels of participation depends on the concept of political participation one is using. Defining, or rather redefining, participation in a way that encapsulates its gradual expansion is therefore the key for setting unambiguous boundaries to the concept as well as for updating our common vocabulary in political science.

The expansion of participation creates the problem of deciding what to consider as participation, while, at the same time, avoiding to fall into the trap of considering everything as participation (van Deth 2001). In light of this dilemma, our first goal is to provide a unified conceptual framework of political participation that allows for confronting this tricky problem in a systematic way. Our objective is not to render traditional definitions obsolete. It is rather to show how the systematic use of elements embedded in different understandings of participation can help us establish a set of rules, through which activities of an unclear political nature can be tested against strict definitional criteria before they are classified for further use as political participation (van Deth 2014; van Deth 2016). The resulting framework provides a vocabulary that helps researchers to arrive at commonly agreed aspects that can be integrated in the systematic study of participation. This approach does not solve the problem of which participatory acts *should* make up a researcher's definitive list. Indeed, it doesn't even aim to do that. It allows, however, for classifying activities of uncertain political nature as political (or not), letting the empirical record judge their prevalence and importance, and thus whether they are phenomena worthy of further investigation. The framework, then, provides a systematic device to deal with the most pressing conceptual challenge: Would you recognize a form of participation if you saw one?

1.2.3 Political Participation Expanded: Methodological and Empirical Issues

Widely used comparative surveys such as the *World Values Survey* (WVS) and the *European Social Survey* (ESS) measure political participation with only a few items, mainly reflecting well-established forms of participation. With a conceptual framework in hand, a list of activities that sufficiently reflects the variety of ways in which people engage in politics today can be designed for a more sophisticated empirical exploration of political participation. But given the abundance of seemingly non-political activities, how do we deal with the problem of discerning what citizens perceive as part of their political participation repertoire and how to measure it as such?

In light of the innumerable activities that citizens may engage in and perceive as political, our starting point for the empirical exploration of political participation is different to that followed in most studies. We will demonstrate the empirical merits of a new approach in which citizens are initially provided with a similar—but longer—list of forms of participation than what is frequently used in available studies. However, after having framed the topic by going through a list of diverse measures of political participation, we continue with an open-ended question that strategically extracts information regarding ways of engagement that involve self-expressive and creative elements, and are above and beyond the forms people usually asked about in surveys. This integrated use of open and closed questions provides an important way forward in understanding the expansion of participation for four reasons. First, information is collected on a number of known forms of participation that is directly comparable to the results of available studies in this field. Second, the addition of an open-ended question allows for acquiring a list of acts that are based on citizens' self-reporting and not on second-hand reports (such as how, for example, a certain creative act may have been covered and interpreted by a magazine, a newspaper, or a political scientist). This approach allows us to collect data on what *citizens themselves* define as participation. By "filtering" the responses through the framework we propose in this book, we can provide conceptual evidence regarding an act's political nature, and thus determine whether it fits the definition of political participation. Third, with the conceptual evidence in hand, we are then able to create a taxonomy; that is, to empirically determine which political activities emerge as new species in the participatory repertoire, and which are simple additions to pre-existing modes of participation. Finally, we are in a position to investigate whether the determinants of new forms and modes of political participation are similar to acts conventionally considered as participation. By exploring the main antecedents of distinct modes of participation, circumstantial evidence is provided to conclude whether new forms of participation indeed belong to the repertoire of participation.

The taxonomy enables us to face some of the methodological issues involved in the study of new forms of participation, most notably the question of whether these forms or modes are indeed perceived by citizens as elements of a broader repertoire of political participation. What if, for example, the planting of a "seedbomb" in a neighborhood is depicted by the instigator as "a democratic statement and an experiment in re-creating space", as Tristanne Days, 24, said to the *Washington Post* journalist who later characterized it as "civil disobedience with a twist" (The Washington Post 2012)? This goes nowhere close to scholars' understanding of political participation—an issue which highlights the kind of problems that arise from studying participation only through repeated measurements with items that reflect participation as previously defined by scholars, but not necessarily by citizens (Marsh, O'Toole, and Jones 2007). As others have argued, for an increasing number of citizens, avoiding traditional politics is part of a new political reality (Eliasoph 1998). With only a handful of exceptions (Micheletti and McFarland 2010; van Deth 2014), this political reality remains largely undertheorized, poorly conceptualized, and, from an empirical point of view, uncharted territory.

1.3 Plan of the Book

In order to deal with the theoretical, conceptual, methodological, and empirical issues of participation research in a rapidly changing world, we developed a strategy to answer the five questions presented in Section 1.1. As can be seen in Figure 1.1, we start our attempts to meet these challenges by a corresponding two-way approach. In Chapter 2 we discuss the problems encountered in empirical studies and the opportunities and limitations presented by the methodologies and instruments currently in use (Question 1). These opportunities and limitations, however, need to be handled before an empirical solution to the problems can be considered. For this reason, we continue with the second main challenge in the next two chapters. In Chapter 3 we study the definitional and conceptual problems encountered in participation research (Question 2), immediately followed in Chapter 4 by the presentation of the solution we propose. Based on the conclusions of Chapters 3 and 4, we then return to solving the crucial problem of dealing with the

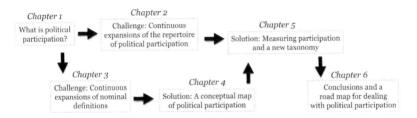

Figure 1.1 Plan of the book

continuously expanding repertoire of political participation in empirical research in Chapter 5 (Questions 3a and 3b). The concluding Chapter 6 summarizes the main conclusions and presents a "road map" for participation research (Question 4).

Our first task—to be dealt with in Chapter 2—is to show how and why (1) the repertoire, (2) the level, and (3) the scope of political participation are changing in democratic societies. A brief summary of empirical evidence on participation from major surveys shows large cross-national differences accompanied by relative stable levels of participation. On the other hand, the results of a number of other empirical studies—usually case studies—on the spread of internet-enabled or internet-boosted forms of participation show rapid changes in many countries. These distinct empirical results clearly corroborate the direct dependency of conclusions about the development of political participation on the methodologies and instruments used—underlining *the need for empirical improvements*.

Conventional conceptualizations of political participation do not cover the continuous expansions of the repertoire of participation. In Chapter 3 we start with an overview of available definitions of participation and spell out the main reasons why older definitions have become less appropriate. Based on a concise literature review of the concept of participation following the landmark studies on voting behavior since the 1940s, a number of recent examples—especially individualized and internet-based forms of participation—are discussed to show that newer activities, such as those enabled by social media, obviously are forms of political participation too. These results all underline *the need for conceptual improvements*.

To deal with the challenges presented in the first chapters, a fresh approach to study political participation is suggested in Chapter 4. Instead of expanding available nominal or functional definitions yet again, a *conceptual map of participation* is developed. This approach allows us to include available definitions in a set of decision rules systematically, efficiently, and consistently. Furthermore, the endless expansions of political participation are covered without excluding any mode of political participation unknown yet. Advantages—and criticism—of this new approach are dealt with by running through the map a number of examples of new forms of participation. A table with "conceptual" evidence as to how each one of those forms fit different definitions of participation concludes this chapter.

Equipped with the conceptual map which allows us to identify diverse activities as forms of political participation, in Chapter 5 we propose a new approach to measure political participation, including both conventional and new forms. For this new approach, a standardized set of items is expanded with an open-ended question on non-political activities used for political purposes. Using data from a survey among a representative sample of the German population we obtained a taxonomy of political activities. After using the conceptual map to evaluate whether these acts fit different definitions of political participation, we empirically examine their place within the broader structure of participation and their main antecedents. Our findings underline the need to use a broad conceptualization of political participation when dealing with changes in democratic societies: Whereas individualized forms of participation can be seen as expansions of existing protest modes of participation, we find that new, digitally networked forms of participation establish a new mode of participation. Furthermore, the taxonomy enables us to estimate how widespread new forms of political participation are, and who uses them—and to put these findings into perspective by comparing the results with similar information for other political activities.

How can our approach and findings be used when studying new forms of political participation without excluding more conventional forms? What problems remain and how can they be addressed? The concluding chapter summarizes the main findings, and answers the five guiding questions we formulated at the end of Section 1.1. Together, these answers present a "road map" with practical suggestions on how to explore political participation in a rapidly changing world (Chapter 6).

Note

1. Although the Does are a fictional family, all the other organizations, persons, and events mentioned in this paragraph are real.

References

The Atlantic. 2015. "Hashtag Activism Isn't a Cop-Out." *The Atlantic.* www.theatlantic.com/politics/archive/2015/01/not-just-hashtag-activism-why-social-media-matters-to-protestors/384215/.

Bang, Henrik P. 2005. "Among Everyday Makers and Expert Citizens." In *Remaking Governance: Peoples, Politics and the Public Sphere*, edited by Janet Newman, 159–78. Bristol: Policy Press.

Barnes, Samuel H, Max Kaase, Klaus R Allerbeck, Barbara G Farah, Felix Heunks, Ronald Inglehart, M Kent Jennings, Hans-Dieter Klingemann, Alan Marsh, and Leopold Rosenmayr. 1979. *Political Action: Mass Participation in Five Western Democracies*. Beverly Hills: Sage.

Berelson, Bernard R, Paul F Lazarsfeld, and William N Mcphee. 1954. *Voting: A Study of Opinion Formation in a Presidential Campaign*. Chicago: University of Chicago Press.

Bite the Ballot. 2017. www.bitetheballot.co.uk.

Blais, André, Elisabeth Gidengil, and Neil Nevitte. 2004. "Where Does Turnout Decline Come From?" *European Journal of Political Research* 43 (2): 221–36.

The Boston Globe. 2014. "Harvard Students Stage 'die-In' to Protest Ferguson, NYC Cases." *The Boston Globe*, December 10. www.bostonglobe.com/metro/2014/12/10/harvard-medical-school-students-stage-die-protest-ferguson-nyc-cases/WeW5pefmWzbTTpgJwVk1KJ/story.html.

CBS News. 2014. "Ferguson Chief: 'Race Relations a Top Priority' Post-Shooting." *CBS News*. www.cbsnews.com/news/ferguson-missouri-police-chief-race-relations-a-top-priority-post-shooting/.

Crouch, Colin. 2004. *Post-Democracy*. Cambridge: Polity Press.

Dalton, Russell. 2008. *The Good Citizen: How a Younger Generation Is Reshaping American Politics*. Washington, DC: CQ Press.

Dalton, Russell, Susan E Scarrow, and Bruce E Cain. 2004. "Advanced Democracies and the New Politics." *Journal of Democracy* 15 (1): 124–38.

Dalton, Russell, and Mark Wattenberg. 2000. *Parties without Partisans: Political Change in Advanced Industrial Democracies*. Oxford: Oxford University Press.

Dalton, Russell, and Christian Welzel. 2014. *The Civic Culture Transformed: From Alegiant to Assertive Citizens*. New York: Cambridge University Press.

Downs, Anthony. 1957. *An Economic Theory of Democracy*. New York: Harper & Row.

Eliasoph, Nina. 1998. *Avoiding Politics: How Americans Produce Apathy in Everyday Life*. Cambridge: Cambridge University Press.

Fieldhouse, Edward, Mark Tranmer, and Andrew Russell. 2007. "Something about Young People or Something about Elections? Electoral Participation of Young People in Europe: Evidence from a Multilevel Analysis of the European Social Survey." *European Journal of Political Research* 46 (6): 797–822.

Franklin, Mark N. 2004. *Voter Turnout and the Dynamics of Electoral Competition in Established Democracies since 1945*. Cambridge: Cambridge University Press.

The Guardian. 2014. "Hypotopia: How a €19bn Model City Has Changed Austria's Attitude to Protest." *The Guardian*, November 11. www.theguardian.com/cities/2014/nov/11/hypotopia-19bn-model-city-changed-austria-attitude-protest.

Harris, Anita, Johanna Wyn, and Salem Younes. 2010. "Beyond Apathetic or Activist Youth: 'Ordinary' Young People and Contemporary Forms of Participation." *Young: Nordic Journal of Youth Research* 18 (1): 9–32.

Hay, Colin. 2007. *Why We Hate Politics*. Cambridge: Polity Press.

Inglehart, Ronald. 1977. *The Silent Revolution: Changing Values and Political Styles among Western Publics*. Princeton: Princeton University Press.

———. 1990. *Culture Shift in Advanced Industrial Society*. Princeton, NJ: Princeton University Press.

———. 2007. "Postmaterialist Values and the Shift from Survival to Self-Expression Values." In *Oxford Handbook of Political Behavior*, edited by Russell Dalton and Hans-Dieter Klingemann, 223–39. New York: Oxford University Press.

Kaase, Max, and Kenneth Newton. 1995. *Beliefs in Government*. Oxford: Oxford University Press.

Lazarsfeld, Paul F, Bernard R Berelson, and Hazel Gaudet. 1948. *The People's Choice: How the Voter Makes Up His Mind in a Presidential Campaign*. New York: Columbia University Press.

Li, Yaojun, and David Marsh. 2008. "New Forms of Political Participation: Searching for Expert Citizens and Everyday Makers." *British Journal of Political Science* 38: 247–72.

Marsh, David, Therese O'Toole, and Su Jones. 2007. *Young People and Politics in the UK: Apathy or Alienaton?* London: Palgrave Macmillan.

Micheletti, Michele. 2003. *Political Virtue and Shopping: Individuals, Consumerism and Collective Action*. New York: Palgrave Macmillan.

Micheletti, Michele, and Andrew S McFarland (eds). 2010. *Creative Participation: Responsibility-Taking in the Political World*. Boulder: Paradigm.

Milner, Henry. 2010. *The Internet Generation: Engaged Citizens or Political Dropouts*. Medford, MA: Tufts University Press.

Morozov, Evgeny. 2009. "The Brave New World of Slacktivism." *Foreign Policy*. http://neteffect.foreignpolicy.com/posts/2009/05/19/the_brave_new_world_of_slacktivism.

Norris, Pippa. 1999. *Critical Citizens: Global Support for Democratic Government*. Oxford: Oxford University Press.

———. 2002. *Democratic Phoenix: Reinventing Political Activism*. Cambridge: Cambridge University Press.

Penney, Joel. 2015. "Social Media and Symbolic Action: Exploring Participation in the Facebook Red Equal Sign Profile Picture Campaign." *Journal of Computer-Mediated Communication* 20 (1): 52–66.

Pharr, Susan J, and Robert D Putnam (eds). 2000. *Disaffected Democracies: What's Troubling the Trilateral Countries?* Princeton: Princeton University Press.

Putnam, Robert D. 2000. *Bowling Alone: The Collapse and Revival of American Community*. New York: Simon and Schuster.

Schlozman, Kay Lehman, Sidney Verba, and Henry E Brady. 2012. *The Unheavenly Chorus: Unequal Political Voice and the Broken Promise of American Democracy*. Princeton: Princeton University Press.

Schudson, Michael. 1998. *The Good Citizen: A History of American Civic Life*. Cambridge, MA: Harvard University Press.

Stoker, Gerry. 2006. *Why Politics Matter: Making Democracy Work*. Houndmills and New York: Palgrave.

Stolle, Dietlind, Marc Hooghe, and Michele Micheletti. 2005. "Politics in the Supermarket: Political Consumerism as a Form of Political Participation."

International Political Science Review/Revue Internationale de Science Politique 26 (3): 245–69.

Torcal, Mariano, and José Ramón Montero (eds). 2006. *Political Dissafection in Contemporary Democracies: Social Capital, Institutions and Politics.* London: Routledge.

van Deth, Jan W. 2001. "Studying Political Participation: Towards a Theory of Everything?" *Joint Sessions of Workshops of the European Consortium for Political Research.* Grenoble.

———. 2014. "A Conceptual Map of Political Participation." *Acta Politica* 49 (3): 349–67.

———. 2015. "Political Participation." In *The International Encyclopedia of Political Communication,* edited by Gianpietro Mazzoleni, Kevin G Barnhurst, Ken'ichi Ikeda, Rousiley C M Maia, and Hartmut Wessler, 1158–69. Hoboken, NJ: John Wiley & Sons, Inc.

———. 2016. "What Is Political Participation." In *Oxford Research Encyclopedia in Politics: Political Behavior.* Oxford: Oxford University Press. politics. oxfordre.com/view/10.1093/acrefore/9780190228637.001.0001/acrefore-9780190228637-e-68.

Verba, Sidney, and Norman H Nie. 1972. *Participation in America: Political Democracy and Social Equality.* Chicago: University of Chicago Press.

The Washington Post. 2012. "'Guerrilla Gardeners' Spread Seeds of Social Change." *The Washington Post.* www.washingtonpost.com/lifestyle/style/2012/04/14/gIQArAA6HT_story.html.

———. 2014. "What Social Media Did for Ferguson." *The Washington Post.* www.washingtonpost.com/news/the-intersect/wp/2014/11/25/what-social-media-did-for-ferguson/?utm_term=.afe88e0227d0.

Wattenberg, Mark. 2002. *Where Have All the Voters Gone?* Cambridge: Harvard University Press.

———. 2008. *Is Voting for Young People?* London: Pearson-Longman.

Welzel, Christian. 2013. *Freedom Rising: Human Empowerment and the Quest for Emancipation.* Cambridge: Cambridge University Press.

2 The Continuous Expansions of Political Participation

> The trends in political activity represent changes in the style of political action, and not just changes in the level of participation.
>
> (Dalton 2008, 94)

2.1 Endless Renewals and Expansions

In the last six decades, the avenues and means for political participation have expanded continuously, by now including such activities as voting, signing petitions, blogging, demonstrating, boycotting products, blocking traffic, joining flash mobs, attending meetings, throwing seedbombs, or donating money.[1] Each of these concrete activities is a *form* of political participation. By increasing the level of abstraction, participation in general can be understood as a latent concept (usually measured as a continuum) that covers more than one form—i.e. it has specific manifestations. A combination of two or more forms of participation sharing some feature is called a *mode* or *type* of participation (we will henceforth use the first one for consistency); for instance, when voting and party activities are depicted together as an electoral mode of participation, or the combination of addressing a question to a politician on Twitter and posting a political video on Facebook as a digitally networked mode. A *repertoire* of political participation unites all available forms—and, therefore, also all modes—of participation affecting politics in a group or society (Tilly 1996). The terms in italics make up the main terminology of participation and can be helpfully thought of as denoting different conceptual and empirical *levels* of participation. Figure 2.1 provides a visual illustration of this vocabulary.

This straightforward vocabulary can be used to specify developments in political participation in the last few decades, avoiding, at the same time, misunderstandings about the exact nature of changes

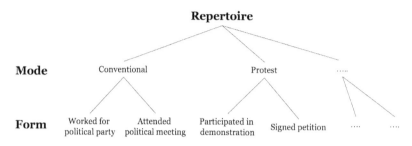

Figure 2.1 The vocabulary of participation: Repertoire, modes, and forms

in participation: The repertoire expanded continuously; that is, new forms of participation were added to existing activities. Much less clear is whether these expansions also imply a rise of new modes of participation. This is because new forms of participation might simply be additions to existing modes, rather than making up an entirely new mode (for instance, when internet-based voting facilities expand the conventional mode of electoral participation they probably do not establish a new mode). Even though it is well-documented that forms of participation have expanded, whether—and in which cases—these expansions imply an enrichment of existing modes or the rise of entirely new modes of participation remains less clear.

Somewhat schematically, the development of political participation can be depicted as the continuous rise of new forms, each of which usually becomes integrated into a new mode of participation in broadly and historically defined "waves". Figure 2.2 depicts this development as a continuous process since the 1940s. In this schematic presentation, each box reflects the available modes of participation at a specific point in time. As long as old forms of participation do not disappear—and they usually do not disappear completely—the repertoire of political participation expands continuously, a trend reflected by arrows traveling towards more recent years. As can be seen on this schema, initially, political participation mainly consisted of voting, but new forms associated with representative political institutions (campaigning, contacting officials) established conventional or institutionalized modes of participation. By the end of the 1960s, new forms (demonstrations, sit-ins, signature actions, etc.) expanded the repertoire, adding a protest mode that included acts that were previously perceived as unconventional, but have since gradually become normalized. The same applies for activities by pacifist or women groups that, in the 1970s and '80s, resulted in a mode of political participation related to

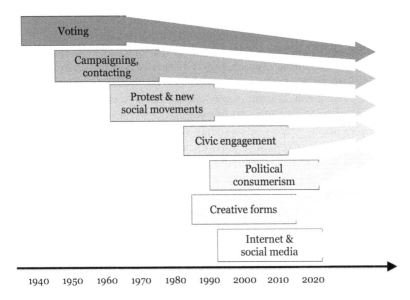

Figure 2.2 The continuous expansions of the repertoire of political participation since the 1940s

new social movements. By the early 1990s the gradually disappearing borderline between political and non-political spheres led to the recognition of a new mode of political participation based on civic activities (volunteering, social engagement, working with others to solve local problems, etc.). Some of the recent expansions that became more popular in the new millennium include forms of participation that reflect a more individualistic style of participation and which are characterized by individual lifestyle preferences and a strong emphasis on the expression of moral and ethical standpoints (boycotting, buycotting). The gamut of participatory acts emerging from lifestyle preferences by now includes some of the most imaginative ways of engaging in politics, such as guerrilla gardening, flash mobs and crowd-initiated public assemblies. Finally, the latest addition to the seemingly never-ending expansion of participation includes forms enabled by the internet—most prominently social media—such as sharing political content or using social media to mobilize others for political purposes.

Whether, and to what extent, newest forms have already resulted in the rise of new modes of participation is debated—the empirical record so far suggests that the use of consumer power to achieve political goals indeed created a new mode of participation ("political consumerism"), whereas some evidence shows the rise of a distinctive type of online participation (Theocharis and van Deth 2016; Gibson and Cantijoch 2013; Teorell, Torcal, and Montero 2007).

Having specified the vocabulary and the main developments in political participation, this chapter presents a concise summary of available empirical evidence documenting its evolution. In the first part, we present results from major longitudinal and cross-national surveys. Evidence from these studies corroborates large cross-national differences accompanied by relatively stable levels of participation in many countries. In the second part, we summarize the results of several studies—usually case studies but also popular accounts—highlighting especially how the spread of new technologies has boosted existing forms of participation or enabled new ones in several countries. These empirical results suggest that conclusions about the development of political participation clearly depend on the methodologies and instruments used. Therefore, in the final section of this chapter we discuss *the need for empirical improvements* resulting from this ambivalent empirical record of participation research.

2.2 Empirical Evidence From Major Surveys

The expansions of the repertoire of participation as schematically depicted in Figure 2.2 were closely observed and identified by scholars in various countries. Empirical political participation research reflects these changes, which can be easily traced with the publication of a number of landmark studies. The seminal voting studies of the 1940s and 1950s focused on voting, campaigning, and party- or election-related activities (Lazarsfeld, Berelson, and Gaudet 1948; Berelson, Lazarsfeld, and McPhee 1954), subsequently expanded with public contacts between citizens and government officials (Campbell et al. 1960). In the late 1960s and early 1970s direct contacts between citizens, public officials, and politicians were included in various studies and so were citizens' cooperative activities (Verba and Nie 1972; Verba, Nie, and Kim 1978). Furthermore, empirical research acknowledged that protesting and actions by new social movements should be accepted as regular political activities (Barnes et al. 1979; Melucci 1989). In a similar way, civic activities such as volunteering and social engagement in all kinds of voluntary associations were accepted as important features of a vibrant civil society (Putnam 1993; Putnam 2000). Recent studies include the use of consumer power (Micheletti 2003; de Moor 2017) as well as the spread of forms of participation that rely on information and communication technologies, and in particular digital media (Earl and Kimport 2011; Bennett and Seger-berg 2013).

Each of these seminal studies not only conceptualized and mea-sured what were—at the time of writing—new forms of participa-tion; each of them also considered these expansions as indicators of the rise of a new mode of participation. This dependency on his-torical developments and specific societal conditions also implies a rather trivial limitation of empirical research: By definition, only existing and recognizable forms of participation are empirically reg-istered at a specific point in time. Whereas, for instance, the results of the Political Action study in the 1970s (Barnes et al. 1979) resulted in the general recognition of protest as an important mode of political participation among political scientists, the results of this extensive study do not offer any clue about political consumerism apart from being involved in "boycotts" as a means of protesting, for the simple reason that buycotts were barely used. Especially large-scale longi-tudinal comparative survey projects such as the WVS or the ESS are constantly under pressure by the conflicting needs of continuity and innovation. On the one hand, change and stability can only be stud-ied when instruments remain the same over time. On the other hand, the rise of new phenomena requires the inclusion of new instruments (Dunleavy 1990).

Although each of these "waves" of expansions has been documented in almost every democratic society (Norris 2002; Teorell, Torcal, and Montero 2007), comparative participation research also shows large differences in the extent and scope of political participation between different countries. As an illustration of the kind of items typically used in this research, we provide here the standard questions on vot-ing, as well as a battery of seven other forms of political participation, that are included in the ESS:[2]

Did you vote in the last [country] national election in [month/year]?

There are different ways of trying to improve things in [country] or help prevent things from going wrong. During the last 12 months, have you done any of the following? Have you . . .

- Contacted a politician or government official
- Worked in a political party or action group
- Worked in another organization or association
- Worn or displayed a campaign badge/sticker
- Signed a petition

- Taken part in a lawful public demonstration
- Boycotted certain products.

Analyses based on the ESS have resulted in a large number of findings about the structure, determinants, antecedents, and consequences of political participation in Europe (Hooghe and Quintelier 2013; Marien, Hooghe, and Quintelier 2010; Roller and Rudi 2008; Sloam 2016). Because all forms of participation are measured with identical items available every two years in the core part of all waves since 2002, the advantages of using these data to study political participation are significant. First, cross-national information for 25 or more countries enables systematic comparisons of political systems with different democratic cultures and historical backgrounds. Second, the repeated cross sections allow for the study of change and stability over time. Third, the general design of the ESS and the use of multiple items to measure political participation enable the application of data-analytic techniques ranging from the construction of scales to measure modes of participation, to regression estimates of longitudinal multilevel models.

Figure 2.3 presents findings for selected forms of participation in 16 European countries that participated in the ESS since its start in 2002. Even a first glance at these results shows large differences in the extent and scope of political participation between different countries: Whereas signing petitions and boycotting products is done by about 40 percent of the population in Sweden, Norway, Finland, France, Germany, Switzerland, and the United Kingdom, these forms of participation are much less popular in Hungary, Poland, Portugal, and Slovenia. These cross-national differences, however, hardly exist for working in a party or action group, or for demonstrating—each attracting less than 10 percent in every country with the exception of Spain. Furthermore, the use of distinct forms of participation varies across time, but these fluctuations are rather modest and concentrated on specific forms of participation in specific countries (for instance, boycotting slowly increases in Sweden, Finland, Germany, and The Netherlands, but remains stable in other countries). In general, substantial cross-national differences co-exist with modest within-country changes in the percentages of citizens being involved in these activities (see references in the previous paragraph for similar conclusions).

In addition to the generally modest changes in participation, several other cross-national similarities can be observed when surveys such as the ESS are used. An important finding relates to the similar structure lying behind the many forms of participation in different countries.

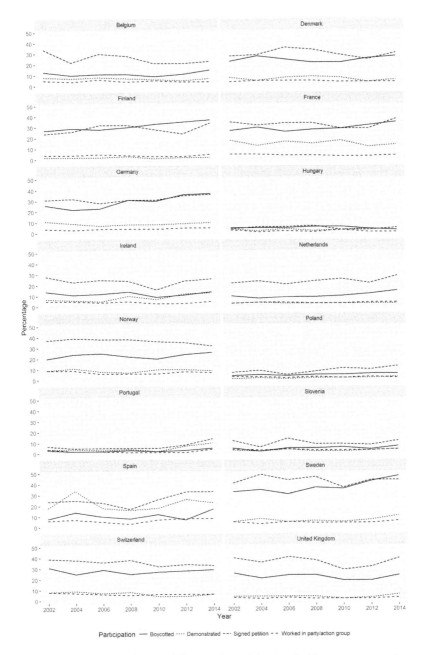

Figure 2.3 The use of several forms of participation in European countries 2002–2014 (percentages "have done"; weighted for design effects)

Source: ESS (Wave 1–7; see note 2)

If constantly emerging new activities are in fact to be regarded as forms of political participation and together form a repertoire, then they need to go together in a latent structure consistently. This is a vital criterion to decide whether arising activities indeed should be accepted as forms of political participation and we will return to this argument when we deal with the interpretation of the results obtained with a new instrument (see Chapter 5). For the moment, it is important to note that the search for such a structure and its persistence have been extensively discussed and several labels have been proposed for the various "types", "dimensions" or "modes" of political participation detected. Dimensional analyses of forms of participation have led to largely consistent results in many countries (Sabucedo and Arce 1991; van Deth 2001). Whereas Milbrath (1965, 18) presented a one-dimensional "pyramid" ranging from active to passive modes of political participation, Milbrath and Goel (1977), and somewhat earlier Verba and Nie (1972), distinguished between four major modes of participation based on more sophisticated empirical analyses: voting, campaign activity, communal activity, and particularized contacting. The distinction Barnes and colleagues (1979) presented between conventional and unconventional modes of political participation is also based on the application of data-reduction techniques to search for latent structure underlying their forms of participation. Applying similar techniques, Parry, Moyser, and Day (1992, 51) found six main types of political participation: voting, party campaigning, collective action, contacting, direct action, and political violence. Finally, Verba, Schlozman, and Brady (1995, 72) categorized political participation in four main activities, broadly labeled as voting, campaign, contact, and community. Since then, others have also found that campaign activities are further decoupled into "campaign" and "contributions" (Glaggett and Pollock 2006, 599).

In all, empirical analyses show that, generally speaking, from the 1960s till about the early 2000s, five distinct modes of participation can be identified: (1) voting, (2) campaign activities, (3) contacting officials or politicians, (4) protest (and new social movements), and (5) social or civic participation. Instead of the outdated distinction between conventional/unconventional modes, many authors now prefer to distinguish between "institutionalized" modes (including modes 1, 2, and 3) and "non-institutionalized" modes of participation (including modes 4 and 5) (Fuchs and Klingemann 1995).

In addition to empirical analyses of latent structures of various forms of participation and the ways they establish distinct modes, typologically oriented approaches have also been presented, such as the typology of political participation developed by the cross-national project Citizenship, Involvement, Democracy (CID) (van Deth, Montero, and Westholm 2007). This two-dimensional typology distinguishes between the channels of influence on the one hand and the mechanisms involved on the other (Teorell, Torcal, and Montero 2007). The first dimension includes forms of participation that refer to channels of representation (such as elections, party activities, or citizens' initiatives) and extra-representative channels (such as product boycotts or attempts to influence public opinion). For the second dimension, citizens can use existing powers (such as elections) or activities that draw attention to certain preferences or interests (such as blockages or petitions). Within this last category some forms of participation are directed to specific actors, groups, or institutions (such as the blockade of a town hall), whereas other activities have no clear addressees and usually try to influence public opinion (such as the publication of future projections). Based on data from the CID study in 12 European countries, Teorell, Torcal, and Montero (2007, 344) show that the typology largely matches the results of the empirical analyses based on the search for latent structure. As this double strategy of conceptual and empirical approaches shows, the major advantage of the typological approach is that it can be used immediately to depict new forms of participation. Confronted with emerging political activities, such as political consumption, Teorell, Torcal, and Montero (2007) included these actions as a new modes of political participation—a finding that had not been recognized by empirical studies up to that point.

Comparative survey research has provided an impressive number of empirically sound conclusions on the spread and development of political participation in many countries over the last decades. Yet its major weakness is implied by its strength: Large-scale, cross-national, and longitudinal data collections require a high degree of harmonization of the instruments used and, therefore, are not ideal to explore the rise of new forms of political involvement. For instance, if your participatory repertoire consists predominantly of dropping seedbombs, participating in creative political poetry slams, and crafting anti-Brexit flash mobs with your friends because you belong to those the *Guardian* identified as "those who reject or ignore the entire political system", then you will not be marked as an activist in most surveys (see also Thorson 2012, 78). Instead, you have a good chance of being depicted as politically disengaged. Furthermore, measures of political participation in such comparative surveys cannot cover upcoming activities that citizens themselves perceive as part of their politically engaged citizenship. This might leave an important gap at a time in which politics becomes increasingly personal and self-reflexive (Bang and Sørensen 1999). What it means to be a politically active citizen for citizens themselves may often be different from scientific definitions—a point raised several times in the literature but which has nevertheless received little empirical attention so far (Marsh, O'Toole, and Jones 2007; Conover, Crewe, and Searing 1991; Eliasoph 1998). This misunderstanding—or rather lack of understanding—comes at a cost of studying political participation in greater depth. As Thorson noted, the way in which people make sense of citizenship—including how they engage in boundary-crossing between what they perceive as personal or private, versus what they see as public or political—matters because "what individuals imagine for and expect of their own civic agency influences civic and political behavior" (2012, 71).

The limitations of standardized surveys are usually acknowledged, but are hardly ever seriously dealt with for more encompassing explorations of new forms of participation. Typical conclusions simply endorse the results obtained with survey data and quantitative analyses, but add only trivial warnings, a simple disclaimer, or a statement of faith without any attempt to deal with this situation:[3]

> [while] manifest, formal and extra-parliamentary political participation are declining [. . .], it might still be possible that this analysis is missing other important forms of political participation.
>
> (Boarini and Díaz 2015, 28)

> Clearly, it would have been preferable to investigate a broader range of participatory acts, but the five ESS items (of the eight recorded in the survey) provide an adequate overview of youth participation in each country.
>
> (Sloam 2016, 5)

For an assessment of changes in participation (and of the quality of democracy), data from the ESS and similar projects are crucial as they offer information that should establish the basis for any serious empirical analysis of political participation. Yet this acknowledgment should not blind us to the fact that longitudinal cross-national surveys provide only a part of the information required to evaluate participation and democracy. Moreover, the main challenge does not seem to be the research strategy applied—several studies use focus groups (Sossou 2011), media analyses (Koopmans and Statham 1999; Francisco 2010), or experimental designs (Levine and Palfrey 2007)—but the selection of specific activities as specimens of political participation.

2.3 Empirical Evidence From Specific Studies

Empirical investigation through the use of surveys into forms of political participation that stretch beyond the classic measures used in cross-national studies is virtually non-existent. This remains the case despite the continuous acknowledgment that new forms of (especially direct) participation (offline or online), may offer part of the cure for the "malaise of representative democracy" (Merkel 2017, 111). A number of scholars, however, have provided exploratory, descriptive, and ethnographic accounts of new avenues of citizen engagement. Probably the most widely studied new forms refer to the use of consumer market power for social and political reasons (Micheletti 2003). Initially, no distinction between boycotting and buycotting was used, but recent empirical evidence suggests that these activities should be distinguished (Copeland 2014; Zorell 2016). Beyond such participation, in her recent book, Lee (2015) explored what she calls "do it yourself politics" or "the public engagement industry"; that is, participatory innovations such as structured deliberations hosted by engagement experts that have emerged to serve governments, and corporate and non-profit clients seeking to listen to citizen demands. Along the same lines, Smith (2009) provided an account of citizen assemblies and mini-publics such as participatory budgeting and direct legislation. Shirky's (2008) popular account emphasizes how the rise of collaborative action, largely facilitated by the internet, has opened up opportunities for voicing opposition or concern to both governments and private institutions in creative ways. Indeed, as illustrated in different studies on "online participatory cultures", participatory opportunities that suit the daily habits and interests of diverse people can emerge in digital environments, ranging from online communities to massively multiplayer online role-playing games and amateur subtitling collectivities (Kahne, Lee, and Feezell 2013; Jenkins 2006; Beyer 2014; Pérez-González 2013). Although these exemplary studies all deal with new avenues of citizen engagement, they only cover a selection of activities—or a selection of specialized communities—for obvious reasons: It is hardly possible to identify the participants and systematically explore incidental and partly anonymous activities such as flash mobs, guerilla gardening or reclaim-the-street parties.[4]

Contrary to the lack of research on offline creative forms of participation which are difficult to detect, a very sizeable amount of studies has empirically investigated forms of participation that rely on digital means. Due to its increasing societal prevalence, the exploration of participation using these means is now an important line of research on participation (Boulianne 2009; Boulianne 2015). Yet the problem of arriving at a common definition of participation has plagued research on this topic. To start with, forms of participation that rely—in one way or another—on the internet have been given such names as "media participation" (Bucy and Gregson 2001), "e-participation" (Macintosh 2008; Gibson and Cantijoch 2013), "online participation" (Saglie and Vabo 2009; Ward, Gibson, and Lusoli 2003; Theocharis 2011), "digital participation" (Bakker and de Vreese 2011; Mercea 2011), "internet participation" (Weber, Loumakis, and Bergman 2003; Krueger 2002), "digitally networked participation" (Theocharis 2015), or "cyber participation" (Steinberg 2015). These concepts are used, sometimes loosely and sometimes with some level of conceptual detail, to refer to forms of participation that are either supported by (specific platforms that rely on) the internet (i.e. signing online petitions) or enabled by it (such as tweeting a message to a politician) (see Earl and Kimport 2011; Van Laer and Van Aelst 2010). This difference is fundamental, as it effectively leads different scholars to studying different activities and calling them a variety of names. Even more importantly, if an act is internet-supported, it means it already existed offline prior to the arrival of this particular technology and thus "merely" provides a low-cost online equivalent. If, on the other hand, it is *enabled* by the internet or an internet-based platform, then it can be thought of as a new way of engaging in politics altogether. Before proceeding to existing empirical evidence regarding the prevalence of these two variants, it is therefore useful to first focus on attempts made by various scholars to empirically differentiate between them.

In their study on how young people combine online and offline civic activities in modes of participation, Hirzalla and van Zoonen (2010) used confirmatory factor analysis on nine offline activities (including both institutionalized acts, such as working for a party, and civic acts, such as doing voluntary work), seven activities aimed at looking up information online, and four online activities such as discussing politics in a forum and signing an online petition. In their analysis, offline institutionalized activities such as working for a party converged with online activities aimed at looking up information about politics, whereas more active forms, such as participating in a demonstration and doing voluntary work, converged with visiting websites of activist organizations. Offline political discussion also converged with online acts such as forwarding emails and engaging in online discussions. The main message of the study was that online participation was not isolated from offline activities. In other words, no such thing as an online mode of political participation was found that was independent from offline activities.

Using a different design but with an eye on a similar question—i.e. to determine whether online participation is distinct from offline activities—Oser, Hooghe, and Marien (2013) used latent-class analysis to examine data from a 2008 American survey. Oser, Hooghe, and Marien (2013, 99) concluded that "a distinct group of activists is drawn to specialize in online versus offline repertoires of political participation, indicating that online political activities are not exclusively the purview of those who are most active in traditional offline activities". Another study that builds on the previous two works was conducted by Gibson and Cantijoch (2013) who subjected data from the 2010 UK general election to confirmatory factor analysis. The authors found that, just as it is the case with offline participation, online participation can be differentiated into distinct clusters (modes) of interrelated activities. Some of these forms correspond directly to offline participatory acts such as contacting politicians and signing petitions, and are thus integrated in existing well-known clusters (or modes). Yet other forms of engagement, notably more expressive ones carried out through Web 2.0 tools such as social networking sites, tend to be independent from offline acts.

The three studies provide important groundwork for understanding online participation and underline the importance of paying attention to the selection of items to measure forms of online and offline participation. Yet a key distinction can be observed when looking at the first and third study. Whereas the first study by Hirzalla and van Zoonen (2010) found that online and offline forms tend to cluster together, their study did not consider participation that relies on Web 2.0-based platforms and applications, such as social networking sites (e.g. Facebook) and microblogs (e.g. Twitter). These are highly interactive applications that rely on a "social" architecture that is much different from the passive architecture of the pre-Web 2.0 era.[5] Thus, as others have noted, they come with an entirely new set of "affordances" (Earl 2014; Chadwick 2014; Halpern and Gibbs 2013; Enjolras, Steen-Johnsen, and Wollebaek 2013; for a detailed discussion see Evans et al. 2017). With this in mind, it is not surprising that Gibson and Cantijoch, who *did* use a limited number of expressive items that rely on Web 2.0 tools (social media in this case) that were absent from the study by Hirzalla and van Zoonen, found that it is exactly acts enabled by these tools that tend to be independent from offline or other online acts. This last finding is crucial because it implies that it may be precisely this kind of digital technologies—and their distinct affordances—that offer entirely new opportunities for engagement with politics.

To provide examples of the prevalence of some online forms of participation in different societies, we focus on a limited number of studies and on the landmark studies by the Pew Research Center (PEW) in the US.[6] On the outset, it is clear that the evolution of survey items in this area is in no way similar to the gradual expansion that we documented for offline participation in the previous section. Moreover, a crucial thing needs to be kept in mind here. As two meta-analyses on the topic (Boulianne 2015; Boulianne 2009) show, research exploring internet or social media use on the one hand, and offline participation on the other, has overwhelmingly focused on the question of how the first influences the second. In other words, the use of internet or social media (operationalized in various ways ranging from the intensity of use, use for acquiring news, use for building networks, etc.) has been generally seen as an independent variable with expected effects on different forms of offline participation—the dependent variable.[7] As such, less emphasis has been laid on online participation as a dependent variable. Already early in their discussions, Gibson and colleagues commented on the tendency of some studies to mis-specify the online political participation variable and noted that:

> Aside from failing to provide any theoretical argument as to why Internet use per se would increase the likelihood of offline participation these studies fail to capture the new and wider range of behaviors involved in online participation. While some participatory opportunities in the online environment do have corollaries in the offline world such as contacting or political discussion, the context provided by the Internet means that the activities take on new dimensions and forms that are at once more visual, immediate, self-selected and impersonal. Examples might be sending e-postcards or political jokes to friends from websites, downloading campaign software, forwarding an online petition or signing up for an e-news bulletin.
>
> (2005, 566)

This observation about what was conceptually missing in the study of online participation, however, did not reverberate in the literature at the time. In 2008 Mossberger and colleagues, while discussing how the internet fosters participation in their pioneering book on digital citizenship, only listed three ways, none of which implied any benefits of internet-enabled participation:

by offering information to help make informed decisions and promote discussion, by supplying outlets such as chat rooms that permit individuals to meet and discuss politics, and by providing interest groups, candidates and parties a means for revitalizing the mobilization efforts of earlier eras through email.

(2008, 89)

Two years later Gil de Zúñiga and colleagues (2010, 38) again pointed out that "current conceptualizations of online political participation typically do not consider behaviors such as displaying campaign slogans on personal Web sites, signing up for a political newsletter, or signing and forwarding an online petition". Boulianne's comment in her 2015 meta-analysis captures precisely the kind of inconsistencies in the measurement of political participation this book is trying to address:

> The bulk of research uses composite indexes that combine very different activities. For example, participation in a demonstration or march is included with measures such as talking to public officials and other measures. [. . .] Furthermore, others do not see any distinction between participating in a demonstration and voting, and therefore use an index that combines both [. . .]. As another example, researchers combine participation in marches or demonstrations in a scale with volunteering for a political party.
>
> (2015, 534)

With these warnings in mind, we draw here on empirical research that has actually used measurements for *some* version of online participation and, more specifically, we rely on a selection of studies that have inclusive batteries. Other studies usually employ selections or variations of the items we document below.

In one of the first studies on online participation in the pre-Web 2.0 era, Krueger (2002, 483) used data from the 2000 US-presidential campaign to sum up six forms and to create an online participation scale (percentages of internet population who have carried them out in brackets):

1. Electronic interpersonal campaign communication (19.2 percent).
2. Contact a candidate online (7.7 percent).
3. Register preferences in an online campaign opinion poll (17.2 percent).
4. Place a campaign hyperlink on a Website (2.9 percent).

5. Visit a candidate's Website (22.8 percent).
6. Donate money to a candidate or political party online (2.0 percent).

With some variations in wording, these items were used by other scholars. Several of those scholars further enriched this list, by either adding more offline items that could be converted online, or by listing other possibilities available on political websites such as "sending an e-postcard from a political organization's website" or "downloading software (screensavers, etc.) from a political organization's website" (Gibson, Lusoli, and Ward 2005, 568). The landscape started to change after the flourishing and proliferation of Web 2.0 applications (approximately 2008), upon which new items were added to that list as various forms of engaging with politics became available through applications such as social networking sites and microblogs. Contrary to offline participation, whereby activities usually do not disappear entirely after they become out of fashion, internet-enabled participation seems to have had such an effect as activities relying on the more interactive Web 2.0 platforms came to replace others that relied on the more passive architecture of the early world wide web. In one of the first studies in the field that systematically assessed the prevalence of online participation in the Web 2.0 era, PEW researchers teamed up with Kay Lehman Schlozman, Sidney Verba, and Henry Brady—commonly acknowledged as key figures in political participation literature—to build and test a battery of questions for these purposes. With these data, Rainie and colleagues (2012) and Smith (2013) considered the percentage of Americans who had done a number of different acts based on social media. Specifically, respondents were asked whether "they had ever used social networking sites or Twitter to . . ." (percentage of adults who have done this in brackets) (Smith 2013, 3):

1. Like or promote material related to political/social issues that others have posted (23 percent).
2. Encourage other people to vote (21 percent).
3. Post their own thoughts/comments on political or social issues (20 percent).
4. Repost content related to political/social issues (19 percent).
5. Encourage others to take action on political/social issues that are important to them (19 percent).
6. Post links to political stories or articles for others to read (17 percent).
7. Belong to a group that is involved in political/social issues, or working to advance a cause (12 percent).

8. Follow elected officials, candidates for office or other public figures (12 percent).

As can be clearly seen, this list, too, includes several acts that are direct conversions of formerly offline forms to the online environment, such as belonging to a political action group, or encouraging other people to vote. Yet, acts such as following elected officials, posting comments on political issues to large numbers of people in one's network, and (re)distributing political content to networks of known and unknown others are all activities that do not have an offline equivalent. It is, indeed, hard to imagine how these last activities could possibly materialize offline. Contrary to other studies that consider as participation acts such as reading online newspapers on topics related to politics or public affairs, or reading online blogs commenting on politics or public affairs (Skoric, Ying, and Ng 2009), the study by PEW considers as participation-only actions with evident behavioral manifestations.

This rich battery of items covers both internet supported (or, if one needs to be more specific, social-media supported) and internet-enabled activities, and is thus suitable for measuring different aspects of online participation. Granted that, with some recent exceptions (Feezell 2016), the battery has rarely been used consistently in terms of wording and in terms of the scope of activities. Some of the items, however, have been used in a comparative study of youth online participation by Vromen and colleagues (2016). Moreover, a series of widely cited studies by Gil de Zúñiga and colleagues (Valenzuela, Kim, and Gil de Zúñiga 2012; Gil De Zúñiga, Molyneux, and Zheng 2014; Gil de Zúñiga, Jung, and Valenzuela 2012)—of which some were conducted before, some around the same time, and some after the PEW study mentioned earlier, thus spanning the whole period during which Web 2.0 applications were popularized and gradually embedded in the political repertoire—also considered forms of online participation in the US. In one of the most recent of these studies, respondents were asked to rate how often they used the internet for the following activities (percentages of those who have done) (Gil De Zúñiga, Molyneux, and Zheng 2014, 324):[8]

1. Write to a politician (57 percent).
2. Make a campaign contribution (36 percent).
3. Subscribe to a political listserv (28 percent).
4. Sign up to volunteer for a campaign/issue (24 percent).
5. Write a letter to the editor of a newspaper (28 percent).

Notice that in this case all items consist of online conversions of formerly offline participatory activities. No new, digitally-enabled forms of participation, are included.

Valeriani and Vaccari (2016) have conducted one of the (up to this point) very few studies examining online participation comparatively—in Germany, Italy, and the UK. Although in this case, too, the emphasis is clearly on formerly offline political activities which have moved online, the comparative aspect allows us to observe the frequency by which these acts are encountered in a national context outside the US. Several items were included in their battery which asked respondents the more general (in the sense that it was about "the Internet" and not about social media specifically) question (Valeriani and Vaccari 2016, 1865):

> Various political activities are carried out via the Internet. During the past 12 months have you . . . ?

- Sent an email to a political leader or party (undertaken by 10.2 percent of German, 15.9 percent of Italian, and 17.9 percent of British respondents)
- Signed an online petition (29.2 percent German, 31.4 percent Italian, and 40.5 percent British)
- Discussed national politics on a forum or blog (14.2 percent German, 19.2 percent Italian, and 21.1 percent British)
- Tried to convince someone to vote for a specific candidate/party/leader using email (6 percent German, 12.5 percent Italian, and 13.4 percent British)
- Used the Internet to involve other people in online and offline political activities (9.2 percent German, 14 percent Italian, and 13 percent British)
- Participated in an offline political activity to which you were invited via the Internet (8.3 percent German, 16.5 percent Italian, and 12.3 percent British)

Finally, in a recent study in the UK, Vaccari, Chadwick, and O'Loughlin (2015, 1052) used an extensive battery of items for political engagement through social media, considering different modes and forms of engagement that rely on the internet or social media. The study questioned a random sample of Twitter users who had posted tweets containing keywords and hashtags related to the European Parliament election, how likely they were (on a scale from 0 to 10) to do the following acts within the next year (percentages of those selecting "10" in brackets):[9]

1. Debate political issues on social media (54.5 percent).
2. Post political news on social media (49.5 percent).
3. Comment on a post by a party/candidate on social media (37.3 percent).
4. Debate politics on a forum or blog (23.5 percent).
5. Use the Internet to encourage other people to take political action (32.4 percent).
6. Encourage someone to vote for a party/candidate via social media (30 percent).
7. Encourage someone to vote for a party/candidate by sending an email (10 percent).

In a similar effort, Gil de Zúñiga, Molyneux, and Zheng (2014, 324) asked their participants if they have done any of the following social media-specific activities on a scale from 0 to 10 (percentages of those who have actually done something in brackets):

1. Posting personal experiences related to politics (34 percent).
2. Friending a political advocate or a politician (35 percent).
3. Posting or sharing thoughts about politics (47 percent).
4. Posting or sharing photos, videos, or audio files about politics (36.5 percent).
5. Forwarding someone else's political commentary to other people (35.5 percent).

Although these studies represent only a fraction of the scholarly work on online participation, an extensive look at the relevant literature demonstrates that the vast majority of studies use either a selection of the aforementioned online political participation items, or some variation of them with slightly amended wordings. This shows the evident lack of consistency in measuring these forms of participation we have highlighted earlier. As demonstrated by the selection, literature relies on a mix of internet-enabled and internet-enhanced activities, of which some actually fall squarely within the definition of political discussion (which political participation research has clearly distinguished from *participation*), and others could even qualify simply as political information gathering.[10] This trend underlines the need for empirical improvements.

2.4 The Need for Empirical Improvements

Political participation has been expanding for several decades, from more conventional, institutionalized forms such as voting and party membership, to non-institutionalized, expressive and creative forms of participation. Empirical research—especially large-scale comparative surveys as the most formidable sources for cross-national and longitudinal analyses of citizens' behavior and attitudes—cannot keep pace with these developments. Comparative surveys such as the ESS and WVS provide important insights by using a battery of items to capture citizens' participatory behavior. Yet these items have remained unchanged since the late 1990s, missing out what may be important new ways in which citizens engage in politics. Crucially, these items operationalize participation exclusively on what scholars define as political participation, and do not consider what citizens perceive as such.

The growing gap between actual participation and scholarly work on citizens' activities has not gone unnoticed (Ekman and Amnå 2012; van Deth 2001). Much of the available work tends to mention as a side note, or indeed as a limitation to current designs, that their empirical work may be overlooking—of failing completely—to study new or emerging forms of participation that are not included in the rigid batteries used in cross-national studies. That being said, the limitation remains exactly that: a limitation or a side note. With few exceptions, there has been virtually no empirical work on what these new and emerging forms of participation look like, and how prevalent they are in societies. When these efforts have been made, they have overwhelmingly focused on forms of participation that rely on the internet and where, interestingly, the problem is reversed (i.e. inconsistency in conceptualizing these types has led to a host of different operationalizations and measures). With the absence of a common understanding, and the lack of a unified approach to the concept of political participation, systematic empirical comparisons of citizens' engagement are largely impossible. These limitations of available empirical studies on participation hamper further scientific work on political activities of ordinary citizens. More importantly, these challenges to empirical research on participation frustrate systematic attempts to understand the quality and health of democracy.

Political participation today may loosely include anything from demonstrating, blog posting and political discussions online and offline, to online iterations of acts that were common already in the 1950s, and entirely new ways that have become available thanks to technological development and digital affordances. How to study political participation empirically when new forms are continuously added to the repertoire? An important part of the answer to this question lies in the way in which we conceptualize and empirically measure participation.

Notes

1. Some of the central driving forces behind the rise of new forms of participation include gradual shifts in citizenship norms and in social and political values in modern societies. Although we have already made a brief mention to these developments in Chapter 1, a full elaboration is beyond the scope of this book, not least because this is a subject of a considerable amount of literature. We refer interested readers to the works of Dalton (2008), Inglehart (1977), and Welzel (2013).
2. All information about the ESS can be found at: www.europeansocialsur vey.org/. See, for a concise project description, Schnaudt et al. (2014).
3. Ironically, many sophisticated quantitative analyses make the study of participation a clear example of what Mead (2010, 454) called "nonempiricism", that is, "what we call research is mostly confined to data analysis" of "data collected by others".
4. Focusing on relatively easily accessible participants at public demonstrations shows the potential of so-called protest surveys (Walgrave and Verhulst 2011) and qualitative interviewing of protesters (Hensel et al. 2015).
5. See, for the affordances of internet applications before and after the Web 2.0 era, O'Reilly (2012) and for the implied paradigm shift on how politics are done online, Earl and Kimport's "Theory 2.0" (2011, 72).
6. See for the studies of PEW: www.pewresearch.org.
7. Studies in the UK, US, and Spain did include forms of online participation but most of them used a very limited number of internet-supported items; more specifically e-donations, e-petitions, and e-contacts (Best and Krueger 2005; Anduiza, Gallego, and Cantijoch 2010; Gibson, Lusoli, and Ward 2005).
8. We are grateful to Homero Gil de Zúñiga for providing us with the exact percentages.
9. We are grateful to Cristian Vaccari, Andrew Chadwick, and Ben O'Loughlin for providing us with material (question wording and percentages) from their study.
10. Several authors are conscious of the difference between participating and discussing or news searching, and opt for the term "online political engagement"; a term that is, however, very broad, inconsistently defined, and rarely covers similar activities across studies.

References

Anduiza, Eva, Aina Gallego, and Marta Cantijoch. 2010. "Online Political Participation in Spain: The Impact of Traditional and Internet Resources." *Journal of Information Technology and Politics* 7 (4): 356–68.

Bakker, Tom P, and Claes H de Vreese. 2011. "Good News for the Future? Young People, Internet Use, and Political Participation." *Communication Research* 38 (4): 451–70.

Bang, Henrik P, and Eva Sørensen. 1999. "The Everyday Maker: A New Challenge to Democratic Governance." *Administrative Theory & Praxis* 21 (3): 325–41.

Barnes, Samuel H, Max Kaase, Klaus R Allerbeck, Barbara G Farah, Felix Heunks, Ronald Inglehart, M Kent Jennings, Hans-Dieter Klingemann, Alan Marsh, and Leopold Rosenmayr. 1979. *Political Action: Mass Participation in Five Western Democracies*. Beverly Hills: Sage.

Bennett, Lance W, and Alexandra Segerberg. 2013. *The Logic of Connective Action: Digital Media and the Personalization of Contentious Politics*. Cambridge: Cambridge University Press.

Berelson, Bernard R, Paul F Lazarsfeld, and William N McPhee. 1954. *Voting: A Study of Opinion Formation in a Presidential Campaign*. Chicago: University of Chicago Press.

Best, Samuel J, and Brian Krueger. 2005. "Analyzing the Representativeness of Internet Political Participation." *Political Behavior* 27 (2): 183–216.

Beyer, Jessica L. 2014. *Expect US: Online Communities and Political Mobilization*. New York: Oxford University Press.

Boarini, Romanini, and Marcos Díaz. 2015. "Cast a Ballot or Protest in the Street—Did Our Grandfathers Do More of Both?" In *OECD Statistics Working Papers*. Paris: OECD Publishing.

Boulianne, Shelley. 2009. "Does Internet Use Affect Engagement? A Meta-Analysis of Research." *Political Communication* 26 (2): 193–211.

———. 2015. "Social Media Use and Participation: A Meta-Analysis of Current Research." *Information, Communication & Society* 18 (5): 524–38.

Bucy, Erik P, and Kimberly S Gregson. 2001. "Media Participation: A Legitimizing Mechanism of Mass Democracy." *New Media & Society* 3 (3): 357–80.

Campbell, Angus, Philip E Converse, Warren E Miller, and Donald E Stokes. 1960. *The American Voter*. New York: John W. Wiley & Sons.

Chadwick, Andrew. 2014. *The Hybrid Media System: Politics and Power*. New York: Oxford University Press.

Conover, Pamela J, Ivor M Crewe, and Donald D Searing. 1991. "The Nature of Citizenship in the United States and Great Britain: Empirical Comments on Theoretical Themes." *Journal of Politics* 53 (3): 800–32.

Copeland, Lauren. 2014. "Conceptualizing Political Consumerism: How Citizenship Norms Differentiate Boycotting from Buycotting." *Political Studies* 62 (1): 172–86.

Dalton, Russell. 2008. "Citizenship Norms and the Expansion of Political Participation." *Political Studies* 56 (1): 76–98.

de Moor, Joost. 2017. "Lifestyle politics and the concept of political participation." *Acta Politica* 56 (2): 179–197.

Dunleavy, Patrick. 1990. "Mass Political Behaviour: Is There More to Learn?" *Political Studies* 38 (3): 453–69.

Earl, Jennifer. 2014. "Something Old and Something New: A Comment on 'New Media, New Civics.'" *Policy & Internet* 6 (2): 169–75.

Earl, Jennifer, and Katrina Kimport. 2011. *Digitally Enabled Social Change: Activism in the Internet Age*. Cambridge: MIT Press.

Ekman, Joakim, and Erik Amnå. 2012. "Political Participation and Civic Engagement: Towards a New Typology." *Human Affairs* 22 (3): 283–300.

Eliasoph, Nina. 1998. *Avoiding Politics: How Americans Produce Apathy in Everyday Life*. Cambridge: Cambridge University Press.

Enjolras, Bernard, Kari Steen-Johnsen, and Dag Wollebaek. 2013. "Social Media and Mobilization to Offline Demonstrations: Transcending Participatory Divides?" *New Media & Society* 15 (6): 890–908.

Evans, Sandra K, Katy E Pearce, Jessica Vitak, and Jeffrey W Treem. 2017. "Explicating Affordances: A Conceptual Framework for Understanding Affordances in Communication Research." *Journal of Computer-Mediated Communication* 22 (1): 35–52.

Feezell, Jessica T. 2016. "Predicting Online Political Participation: The Importance of Selection Bias and Selective Exposure in the Online Setting." *Political Research Quarterly* 69 (3): 495–509.

Francisco, Ronald A. 2010. *Collective Action Theory and Empirical Evidence*. New York: Springer.

Fuchs, Dieter, and Hans-Dieter Klingemann. 1995. "Citizens and the State: A Changing Relationship?" In *Citizens and the State*, edited by Hans-Dieter Klingemann and Dieter Fuchs, 1–23. Oxford: Oxford University Press.

Gibson, Rachel, and Marta Cantijoch. 2013. "Conceptualizing and Measuring Participation in the Age of the Internet: Is Online Political Engagement Really Different to Offline?" *The Journal of Politics* 75 (3): 701–16.

Gibson, Rachel, Weiner Lusoli, and Stephen Ward. 2005. "Online Participation in the UK: Testing a 'Contextualised' Model of Internet Effects." *The British Journal of Politics and International Relations* 7 (4): 561–83.

Gil de Zúñiga, Homero, Nakwon Jung, and Sebastian Valenzuela. 2012. "Social Media Use for News and Individuals' Social Capital, Civic Engagement and Political Participation." *Journal of Computer-Mediated Communication* 17 (3): 319–36.

Gil de Zúñiga, Homero, Logan Molyneux, and Pei Zheng. 2014. "Social Media, Political Expression, and Political Participation: Panel Analysis of Lagged and Concurrent Relationships." *Journal of Communication* 64 (4): 612–34.

Gil de Zúñiga, Homero, Aaron Veenstra, Emily Vraga, and Dhavan Shah. 2010. "Digital Democracy: Reimagining Pathways to Political Participation." *Journal of Information Technology & Politics* 7 (1): 36–51.

Glaggett, William, and Philip H Pollock. 2006. "The Modes of Participation Revisited, 1980–2004." *Political Research Quarterly* 59 (4): 593–600.

Halpern, Daniel, and Jennifer Gibbs. 2013. "Social Media as a Catalyst for Online Deliberation? Exploring the Affordances of Facebook and YouTube for Political Expression." *Computers in Human Behavior* 29 (3): 1159–68.

Hensel, Alexander, Daniela Kallinich, Julia Kiegeland, Robert Lorenz, and Robert Mueller-Stahl. 2015. *Demokratie in Aufruhr*. Stuttgart: ibidem-Verlag.

Hirzalla, Fadi, and Liesbet van Zoonen. 2010. "Beyond the Online/Offline Divide: How Youth's Online and Offline Civic Activities Converge." *Social Science Computer Review* 29 (4): 481–98.

Hooghe, Marc, and Ellen Quintelier. 2013. "Political Participation in Europe." In *Society and Democracy in Europe*, edited by Silke I Keil and Oscar W Gabriel, 220–43. London: Routledge.

Inglehart, Ronald. 1977. *The Silent Revolution: Changing Values and Political Styles among Western Publics*. Princeton: Princeton University Press.

Jenkins, Henry. 2006. *Convergence Culture: Where Old and New Media Collide*. New York: New York University Press.

Kahne, Joseph, Nam-Jin Lee, and Jessica T Feezell. 2013. "The Civic and Political Significance of Online Participatory Cultures among Youth Transitioning to Adulthood." *Journal of Information Technology & Politics* 10 (1): 1–20.

Koopmans, Ruud, and Paul Statham. 1999. "Political Claims Analysis: Integrating Protest Event and Political Discourse Approaches." *Mobilization* 4 (2): 203–21.

Krueger, Brian. 2002. "Assessing the Impact of Internet Political Participation in the United States: A Resource Approach." *American Political Research* 30 (5): 476–98.

Lazarsfeld, Paul F, Bernard R Berelson, and Hazel Gaudet. 1948. *The People's Choice: How the Voter Makes Up His Mind in a Presidential Campaign*. New York: Columbia University Press.

Lee, Caroline W. 2015. *Do-It-Yourself Democracy: The Rise of the Public Engagement Industry*. Oxford: Oxford University Press.

Levine, David K, and Thomas R Palfrey. 2007. "The Paradox of Voter Participation? A Laboratory Study." *American Political Science Review* 101 (1): 143–58.

Macintosh, Ann. 2008. "E-Democracy and E-Participation Research in Europe." In *Digital Government: E-Government Research, Case Studies, and Implementation*, edited by Chen Hsinchun, Lawrence Brandt, Valerie Gregg, Roland Traunmüller, Sharon Dawes, Eduard Hovy, Ann Macintosh, and Catherine A Larson, 85–102. New York: Springer.

Marien, Sofie, Marc Hooghe, and Ellen Quintelier. 2010. "Inequalities in Non-Institutionalised Forms of Political Participation: A Multi-Level Analysis of 25 Countries." *Political Studies* 58 (1). Blackwell Publishing Ltd: 187–213.

Marsh, David, Therese O'Toole, and Su Jones. 2007. *Young People and Politics in the UK: Apathy or Alienaton?* London: Palgrave Macmillan.

Mead, Lawrence M. 2010. "Scholasticism in Political Science." *Perspectives on Politics* 8 (2): 453–64.

Melucci, Alberto. 1989. *Nomads of the Present: Social Movements and Individual Needs in Contemporary Society*. London: Hutchinson.

Mercea, Dan. 2011. "Digital Prefigurative Participation: The Entwinement of Online Communication and Offline Participation in Protest Events." *New Media & Society* 14 (1): 153–69.

Merkel, Wolfgang. 2017. "The Limits of Democratic Innovations in Established Democracies." In *The Governance Report 2017*, 111–26. Oxford: Oxford University Press.

Micheletti, Michele. 2003. *Political Virtue and Shopping: Individuals, Consumerism and Collective Action*. New York: Palgrave Macmillan.

Milbrath, Lester W. 1965. *Political Participation: How and Why Do People Get Involved in Politics*. Chicago: Rand McNally.

Milbrath, Lester W, and Madan L Goel. 1977. *Political Participation: How and Why Do People Get Involved in Politics*. Chicago: Rand McNally.

Mossberger, Karen, Caroline J Tolbert, and Ramona S McNeal. 2008. *Digital Citizenship: The Internet, Society and Participation*. Cambridge: MIT Press.

Norris, Pippa. 2002. *Democratic Phoenix: Reinventing Political Activism*. Cambridge: Cambridge University Press.

O'Reilly, Tim. 2012. "What Is Web 2.0? Design Patterns and Business Models for the Next Generation Software." In *The Social Media Reader*, edited by Michael Mandiberg, 32–52. New York: New York University Press.

Oser, Jennifer, Marc Hooghe, and Sofie Marien. 2013. "Is Online Participation Distinct from Offline Participation? A Latent Class Analysis of Participation Types and Their Stratification." *Political Research Quarterly* 66 (1): 91–101.

Parry, Geraint, George Moyser, and Neil Day. 1992. *Political Participation and Democracy in Britain*. Cambridge: Cambridge University Press.

Pérez-González, Luis. 2013. "Amateur Subtitling as Immaterial Labour in Digital Media Culture: An Emerging Paradigm of Civic Engagement." *Convergence: The International Journal of Research into New Media Technologies* 19 (2): 157–75.

Putnam, Robert D. 1993. *Making Democracy Work: Civic Traditions in Modern Italy*. Princeton, NJ: Princeton University Press.

———. 2000. *Bowling Alone: The Collapse and Revival of American Community*. New York: Simon and Schuster.

Rainie, Lee, Aaron Smith, Kay Lehman Schlozman, Henry E Brady, and Sidney Verba. 2012. "Social Media and Political Engagement." http://pewinternet.org/Reports/2012/Political-engagement.aspx.

Roller, Edeltraud, and Tatjana Rudi. 2008. "Explaining Level and Equality of Political Participation: The Role of Social Capital, Socioeconomic Modernity, and Political Institutions." In *Social Capital in Europe: Similarity of Countries and Diversity of People? Multi-Level Analyses of the European Social Survey 2002*, edited by Heiner Meulemann, 251–84. Leiden: Brill.

Sabucedo, Jose M, and Constantino Arce. 1991. "Types of Political Participation: A Multidimensional Analysis." *European Journal of Political Research* 20 (1): 93–102.

Saglie, Jo, and Signy I Vabo. 2009. "Size and E-Democracy: Online Participation in Norwegian Local Politics." *Scandinavian Political Studies* 32 (4): 382–401.

Schnaudt, Christian, Michael Weinhardt, Rory Fitzgerald, and Stefan Liebig. 2014. "The European Social Survey: Contents, Design, and Research Potential." *Schmollers Jahrbuch* 134 (4): 487–506.

Shirky, Clay. 2008. *Here Comes Everybody: The Power of Organizing without Organizations*. New York: Penguin.

Skoric, Marko M, Deborah Ying, and Ying Ng. 2009. "Bowling Online, Not Alone: Online Social Capital and Political Participation in Singapore." *Journal of Computer-Mediated Communication* 14: 414–33.

Sloam, James. 2016. "Diversity and Voice: The Political Participation of Young People in the European Union." *The British Journal of Politics and International Relations* 18 (3): 521–37.

Smith, Aaron. 2013. "Civic Engagement in the Digital Age." http://pewinternet.org/Reports/2013/Civic-Engagement.aspx.

Smith, Graham. 2009. *Democratic Innovations: Designing Institutions for Citizen Participation*. Cambridge: Cambridge University Press.

Sossou, Marie-Antoinette. 2011. "We Do Not Enjoy Equal Political Rights: Ghanaian Women's Perceptions on Political Participation in Ghana." *SAGE Open*. journals.sagepub.com/doi/10.1177/2158244011410715.

Steinberg, Alan. 2015. "Exploring Web 2.0 Political Engagement: Is New Technology Reducing the Biases of Political Participation?" *Electoral Studies* 39: 102–16.

Teorell, Jan, Mariano Torcal, and José Ramón Montero. 2007. "Political Participation: Mapping the Terrain." In *Citizenship and Involvement in European Democracies: A Comparative Analysis*, edited by Jan W van Deth, José Ramón Montero, and Anders Westholm, 334–57. London: Routledge.

Theocharis, Yannis. 2011. "Young People, Political Participation and Online Postmaterialism in Greece." *New Media & Society* 13 (2): 203–23. doi:10.1177/1461444810370733.

———. 2015. "The Conceptualization of Digitally Networked Participation." *Social Media + Society* 1 (2): 1–14.

Theocharis, Yannis, and Jan W van Deth. 2016. "The Continuous Expansion of Citizen Participation: A New Taxonomy." *European Political Science Review*. https://goo.gl/lYJtk7.

Thorson, Kjerstin. 2012. "What Does It Mean to Be a Good Citizen? Citizenship Vocabularies as Resources for Action." *The ANNALS of the American Academy of Political and Social Science* 644 (1): 70–85.

Tilly, Charles. 1996. *Popular Contention in Great Britain, 1758–1834*. Cambridge, MA: Harvard University Press.

Vaccari, Cristian, Andrew Chadwick, and Ben O'Loughlin. 2015. "Dual Screening the Political: Media Events, Social Media, and Citizen Engagement." *Journal of Communication* 65 (6): 1041–61.

Valenzuela, Sebastian, Yonghwan Kim, and Homero Gil de Zúñiga. 2012. "Social Networks That Matter: Exploring the Role of Political Discussion for Online Political Participation." *International Journal of Public Opinion Research* 24 (2): 163–84.

Valeriani, Augusto, and Cristian Vaccari. 2016. "Accidental Exposure to Politics on Social Media as Online Participation Equalizer in Germany, Italy, and the United Kingdom." *New Media & Society* 18 (9): 1857–74.

van Deth, Jan W. 2001. "Studying Political Participation: Towards a Theory of Everything?" *Joint Sessions of Workshops of the European Consortium for Political Research*. Grenoble.

van Deth, Jan W, José Ramón Montero, and Anders Westholm (eds). 2007. *Citizenship and Involvement in European Democracies: A Comparative Analysis*. London: Routledge.

Van Laer, Jeroen, and Peter Van Aelst. 2010. "Internet and Social Movement Action Repertoires." *Information, Communication & Society* 13 (8): 1146–71.

Verba, Sidney, and Norman H Nie. 1972. *Participation in America: Political Democracy and Social Equality*. Chicago: University of Chicago Press.

Verba, Sidney, Norman H Nie, and Jae-On Kim. 1978. *Participation and Political Equality: A Seven-Nation Comparison*. New York and London: University of Chicago Press.

Verba, Sidney, Kay Lehman Schlozman, and Henry E Brady. 1995. *Voice and Equality: Civic Voluntarism in American Politics*. Cambridge: Harvard University Press.

Vromen, Ariadne, Brian D Loader, Michael A Xenos, and Francesco Bailo. 2016. "Everyday Making through Facebook Engagement: Young Citizens Political Interactions in Australia, the United Kingdom and the United States." *Political Studies* 64 (3): 513–33.

Walgrave, Stefaan, and Joris Verhulst. 2011. "Selection and Response Bias in Protest Surveys." *Mobilization* 16 (2): 203–22.

Ward, Stephen, Rachel Gibson, and Weiner Lusoli. 2003. "Online Participation and Mobilisation in Britain: Hype, Hope and Reality." *Parliamentary Affairs* 56 (4): 654–68.

Weber, Lori M, Alysha Loumakis, and James Bergman. 2003. "Who Participates and Why? An Analysis of Citizens on the Internet and the Mass Public." *Social Science Computer Review* 21 (1): 26–42.

Welzel, Christian. 2013. *Freedom Rising: Human Empowerment and the Quest for Emancipation*. Cambridge: Cambridge University Press.

Zorell, Carolin. 2016. "Varieties of Political Consumerism." PhD Dissertation. Universität Mannheim, Germany. ub-madoc.bib.uni-mannheim.de/42488.

3 The Continuous Expansions of Concepts and Definitions of Political Participation

> Those with the most restrictive and conventional conceptions of political participation identify a strong and consistent pattern of declining political participation and engagement over time, whilst those with a more inclusive conception discern instead a change in the *mode* of political participation.
>
> (Hay 2007, 23; italics in original)

3.1 Endless Renewals and Expansions

The continuous expansions of the repertoire of participation have been followed by corresponding expansions of concepts and definitions of political participation. Whereas several authors rely on inductive approaches and simply add new forms of participation to existing enumerations of available forms, others have expanded nominal definitions in order to cover a broader array of activities. In this chapter, we start with an overview of available definitions of participation and spell out the main reasons why older definitions have become obsolete. Based on a brief literature review beginning with the landmark studies on voting behavior since 1948, we show that, gradually, scholars' attention shifted from institutionalized acts that are usually based on specific institutional or constitutional arrangements (such as voting, which is carried out at scheduled times in elections), to acts initiated by citizens (which vary depending on political and cultural settings). Subsequently, we account for further expansions of the definition of political participation which adopt a broader perspective in order to capture diverse forms of engagement based on social and lifestyle activities that have no direct links to the political arena. To this end, we deal with recent examples of such participation, focusing especially on individualized forms of collective action and internet-based (more specifically social-media based) forms of participation. These examples show that many such activities are initiated and pursued eagerly by citizens as politically meaningful participation, although they do not fit available, especially conventional, definitions of the concept.

The chapter discusses the advantages of understanding new forms of political participation and argues that existing conceptualizations lead to the pitfalls of either missing out on emerging forms of political engagement, or risking considering everything as participation. To deal with this dilemma pragmatically, the most important task is to avoid ending up with a "concept of everything"; that is, with a definition of participation that does not allow for a clear demarcation between forms of political participation on the one hand, and other specimen of human behavior on the other.

3.2 Available Concepts and Definitions

A virtually endless list of conceptualizations and definitions of political participation follows the continuous expansions of the repertoire of political participation (Brady 1999; Conge 1988; Fox 2013; van Deth 2001). To mention only some of the most widely used conceptualizations, political participation is defined as:

> those actions of private citizens by which they seek to influence or to support government and politics.
>
> (Milbrath and Goel 1977, 2)

> those activities by private citizens that are more or less directly aimed at influencing the selection of governmental personnel and/or the actions they take.
>
> (Verba and Nie 1972, 2)

> all voluntary activities by individual citizens intended to influence either directly or indirectly political choices at various levels of the political system.
>
> (Kaase and Marsh 1979a, 42)

> 'taking part in the process of formulation, passage and implementation of public policies'. It is concerned with action by citizens which is aimed at influencing decisions which are, in most cases, ultimately taken by public representatives and officials. This may be action which seeks to shape the attitudes of decision-makers to matters yet to be decided, or it may be action in protest against the outcome of some decision.
>
> (Parry, Moyser, and Day 1992, 16)

activities of citizens that attempt to influence the structure of government, the selection of government authorities, or the policies of government. These activities may be supportive of the existing policies, authorities, or structure, or they may seek to change all of these. This definition emphasizes active involvement that is instrumental or goal-oriented. However, political participation also includes passive kinds of involvement, such as attending ceremonial or supportive activities, or paying attention to what is happening in the government or in politics.

(Conway 1991, 13)

affords citizens in a democracy an opportunity to communicate information to government officials about their concerns and preferences and to put pressure on them to respond.

(Verba, Schlozman, and Brady 1995)

any dimensions of activity that are either designed directly to influence government agencies and the policy process, or indirectly to impact civil society, or which attempt to alter systematic patterns of social behavior.

(Norris 2001, 16)

all forms of involvement in which citizens express their political opinion and/or convey that opinion to political decision-makers.

(Vissers and Stolle 2014, 937)

Although they emphasize distinct aspects differently, a common understanding of, at least, a fundamental idea of what constitutes political participation is evident from these quotations (van Deth 2014; van Deth 2001). First, political participation refers to people in their role as *citizens* and not, say, as politicians or civil servants. Second, with the exception of the definition by Conway which also allows for "passive" participation (a topic which many scholars—including ourselves—take issue with), political participation is understood as an *activity* ("action")—simply watching television or claiming to be curious about politics does not constitute political participation. Nor does showing an interest in politics by reading the news, or talking about it with friends or family qualify as participation, as Parry, Moyser, and Day (1992, 16) have pointed out. Third, the activities of citizens we define as political participation should be *voluntary* and not ordered by a ruling class or obliged under some law or decree. Finally, political participation concerns *government and politics* in a broad sense of these words ("political system") and is neither restricted to specific phases (such as parliamentary decision-making, or the input side of the political system), nor to specific levels or areas (such as national elections or contacts with officials). These four features of political participation are included or implied in almost every available definition and are therefore largely undisputed.

Various examples that have been provided so far in this book make it obvious that these criteria do not suffice for capturing what citizens perceive today as political participation. Several scholars have noted, for example, that citizens increasingly consider the expression of opinions in different contexts, to different audiences, and with different tools, as a form of political participation. In their study of online expressive participation, Rojas and Puig-I-Abril (2009) offer one of the clearest accounts of how public expressiveness can be perceived as political participation. Expressive political participation, they argue, is "a form of political participation that entails the public expression of political orientations" (Rojas and Puig-I-Abril 2009, 906). They are careful to not blur the distinction between political conversation and expressive political participation like others have opted for (Boyle et al. 2006), pointing out that "not all political conversations entail participatory behavior. It is clear to us that all forms of political conversation have important political consequences, but distinguishing between background conversations and the public expression of our views makes sense theoretically and has been supported empirically" (Rojas and Puig-I-Abril 2009, 907). Apparently, the first three basic criteria specified in the previous paragraph—citizens; activity; voluntary—still apply, but the required orientation towards politics and government is much more broadly understood.

Expressing views is not limited to political conversations. An important part of politics today is "channelled through often dense social networks over which people can share their own stories and concerns— the pervasive use of social technology enables individuals to become important catalysts of collective action processes as they activate their own social networks" (Bennett 2012, 22). A manifestation of such a form of participation is digitally networked participation (DNP), a continuously growing opportunity for citizen engagement (Theocharis 2015). That this type of participatory behavior falls short of the criteria required for a basic definition of participation enumerated above has been noted by Schlozman and colleagues:

> Many forms of political engagement in these venues do not fall squarely under the rubric of a definition of political participation

as 'activity that has the intent or effect of influencing government action—either directly by affecting the making or implementation of public policy or indirectly by influencing the selection of people who make those policies'.

(2012, 532)

The act of tweeting a message or an image about the death of an unarmed black man by a white policeman fails the criterion of taking place within the area in which government and politics (or even broadly the political system) are practiced, and so does "liking" a candidate's Facebook page, or embedding a symbol in one's social-media profile picture in solidarity with a social movement. As these acts can be done from one's living room lying in front of the TV, for many scholars they simply don't even qualify as an activity, and have been famously derided as "slacktivism" (Morozov 2009). Schlozman and colleagues do raise a legitimate concern about the (as of yet not fully understood) political role of such activities:

> Will a social networking site like Facebook facilitate the dissemination of political information and encourage other modes of online and offline political participation, as conventionally understood? Or will these rapidly changing forms of digital interaction dilute the meaning of politically engaged citizenship? Although 'liking' a candidate is not the same as taking part in a campaign, will it become the first step in that direction? Can the political groups formed on a social networking site become the basis for sustained political action as well as an infrastructure for mobilization?
>
> (2012, 533)

Some of the questions raised in this section are gradually being answered. For example, drawing on two panel studies in the US, Kahne, Lee, and Feezell (2013, 1) found that, for young people, interest-driven non-political activity taking place in online venues such as social media can serve as a gateway to participation in civic and political life. Furthermore, thousands of messages were sent and became part of the organization, coordination, and sustained mobilization of one of the most politically vibrant movements against racism and discrimination since the civil rights movement of the 1960s: Black Lives Matter (see section 1.1 this book) (Freelon, McIlwain, and Clark 2016). Most importantly, organizations (in this and other cases) explicitly encouraged citizens through printed and online material to get involved with the movement through digital means, spread the word, and organize. Sending tweets with images related to the movement even led to higher levels of political mobilization (Casas and Williams 2016). Other research has shown that following a politician on Twitter during an election campaign has a positive impact of feelings towards the candidate (Kobayashi and Ichifuji 2015), which might be the first step towards greater involvement.[1]

The rapid proliferation of social media and their use for political and social purposes shows the increasing complications to distinguish political participation from other phenomena. Apparently, even the question what constitutes an "activity" is challenged (is "liking" an activity?). But very similar discussions took place with almost each wave of expansions of the repertoire of political participation. Several other common characteristics have been proposed and discussed as relevant, or essential, for defining an act as political participation, some of which apply directly to the movement just described:

1. The (il)legal status of activities.
2. The question whether or not the actions have been successful or recognized by political "gate keepers".
3. The elite-directed or elite-challenging nature of activities.
4. A distinction between collective and individual action.
5. The symbolic nature of an act.
6. The personal resource investment required for carrying out the activity (i.e. the cost).
7. The activity's impact.
8. The various motivations of citizens involved.

The list, which is certainly not exhaustive, shows that additional criteria could be—and in fact are—added by scholars, observers, and pundits when it comes to defining political participation. What becomes immediately clear, however, is that consideration of such criteria is likely to increasingly dilute our notion of political participation making it, at the same time, empirically close to impossible to grasp it unambiguously.

Especially the rise of expressive forms of participation, and the spread of social media, considerably expanded the list of additional criteria to be taken into account when defining political participation. Yet many of these conditions are either too difficult to specify unambiguously or impossible to capture—nor can they be identified empirically. One of the most notoriously difficult aspects concerns the last point listed: the motivations of citizens involved. For some, this point even defines the level of success of a particular act. As Zuckerman notes in his critique of slacktivism, "evaluating the success of any online engagement requires asking what a civic actor hoped to achieve and whether she achieved it" (Zuckerman 2014, 163). How do we disentangle, however, whether, for example, a participant took to the streets because of evident political purposes or ideological reasons, or due to a random invitation by her friends, because a person of interest would also attend the protest, or because she was caught by the march while on her way to the cinema? Or is it because of altogether different reasons, such as because she is someone who might seek self-fulfillment and feel that she could gain recognition by her peers, or because she is risk-accepting and finds protests a source of novelty and excitement (for relevant research, see Kam 2012)?[2]

Two of the most vibrantly contested issues in this debate—and the core issues behind the gradually fading discussion about slacktivism—are the costs and success/impact of the activity. With regards to costs: One has to stress that participation requiring a small amount of effort, such as sharing a political opinion on social media, may be a low-cost activity in Germany or the UK, but may be enough to get you in prison for several months (or worse) in Egypt or China (MacKinnon 2013). The question of the impact of internet-enabled acts, raised forcefully by Morozov (2009), is another turn to a tricky territory whereby things aren't as obvious as they seem (i.e. low cost does not necessarily imply "zero impact", as Morozov argues). Already before the arrival of the internet outcomes have been neither easy nor straightforward to measure (for detailed discussions see Earl 2000; Biggs and Andrews 2015). At the same time, in the age of social media simply sharing a call for action has been shown to be critical for increasing the reach of a campaign's message (Barberá et al. 2015), leading to certain initiatives getting picked up by the media, eventually reaching, and reportedly having a lasting effect on, the government's policy agenda (Time 2016). Whereas their legacy and nature of success remains a matter of debate, Occupy Wall Street, KONY 2012, Bring Back our Girls, Black Lives Matter, Stuttgart 21, and the #IF Campaign are only some entries in a long list of "crowd-" and "organizationally-enabled" connective action campaigns (Bennett and Segerberg 2013, 47) that elevated the issues advocated to the center of the policy agenda while relying on, and benefiting from, precisely this kind of participation (Tufekci 2012; Tufekci 2014; Jungherr and Jürgens 2014; Sajuria et al. 2015). As Karpf (2010, 9) has pointed out, low-cost online activities (such as re-distributing an image on Twitter or forwarding an organization's petition to your colleagues), are often a small component of broader campaign's action repertoire and strategy aimed at influencing public decision-makers. Seeing these acts as if they are occurring in a vacuum, and condemning them as couch-potato participation (or, even worse, non-participation—see Morozov 2013, 5), disregards the broader (strategic) context in which they are embedded, and thus something that can define their power (Karpf 2016), as well as their political utility (see our discussion about the criterion of context in Chapter 4's conceptual map of political participation).

Overall, discrepancies between existing definitions on the one hand, and the range of phenomena to be covered on the other, do not present an entirely new problem. Nor are such complications restricted to the concept of political participation. Yet the radical expansion of seemingly non-political participation (and perhaps the decline of those acts traditionally defined as political participation) has exacerbated the urgency to handle the difficulties encountered when trying to arrive at a common understanding of political participation.

This overview provides us with two main messages. First of all, attempts for redefining participation should, at the very least, recognize the "classic" four baseline criteria enumerated earlier. These criteria are common to almost all—be they narrow or broad—definitions of political participation and establish the core of every understanding of political participation. Second, therefore, although the four common criteria are necessary conditions to define political participation, they certainly do not suffice for dealing with the many activities citizens nowadays engage in, many of which lack a clear political connotation—at least an immediate one. How, then, can we expand our definition of political participation without drowning in an almost endless list of criteria?

3.3 How to Avoid a "Concept of Everything"?

A first way to deal with the complications of defining political participation is simply to deny the need for such an exercise altogether. McCaughey and Ayers (2003, 14), for example, in their pioneering book *Cyberactivism*, note that: "*Cyberactivism* refuses to define the boundaries of online activism or to determine what counts and does not count as legitimate online activism. Defining online activism is as difficult as defining activism before the Internet". As we argued in the introductory chapter, this practice obstructs meaningful evaluations of the quality of democracy and the preconditions for a vibrant democratic system—to say nothing of empirical understandings of the phenomenon. As such, scholars have attempted to deal with this complications in different ways. Three main strategies are presented in the literature—not as explicit attempts to deal with conceptual problems, but as pragmatic ways to define the object under study: (1) expanding the list of participation specimens inductively, (2) modifying nominal definitions, and (3) limiting the scope or sphere of political participation.

3.3.1 Inductive Approaches

The first way to deal with the continuous expansion of participation is to simply expand the list of forms with new activities, when they become available. The drawback of this approach is, of course, that it is as easy as it is impractical. Lacking strict conceptual criteria, scholars are bound to compile lists of interesting phenomena which serve their specific research agendas. The probable outcome is that lists of wildly different phenomena (for example, "looking for political information on the web", "signing an online petition", and "downloading software [screensavers, etc.] from a political organization's website"— see Gibson, Lusoli, and Ward 2005, 568) will be presented as forms of participation, with little consistency across different contexts and, therefore, little comparability. In such cases, scholars often note that they adopt a broad or expansive conception of political participation, and proceed without placing further emphasis on the conceptual question. The most likely, and probably most sensible, outcome of such efforts is that the items used to operationalize new forms of participation will remain the object of interest in small-scale studies in national contexts, with little chances of ever being adopted by large-scale comparative surveys.[3]

   The disadvantages of this approach are most notable if we look at the implications for longitudinal analyses. Even if scholars agree that a new phenomenon establishes an expansion of the repertoire of political participation—as was, for instance, the case with protest activities in the 1970s or civic participation in the 1990s—our definitions have to be updated constantly. The rather impractical effects of expanding definitions inductively are that no unambiguous conclusions about differences in, or persistence and changes of participation across time, can be formulated—apart from the important notion that both political participation in the real world and the theoretical concept expand constantly. In short, endless conceptual additions in an inductive fashion are a problematic response to endless expansions in the real world: It will be only a matter of time before we arrive at a "concept of everything".

3.3.2 Modifying Nominal Definitions

Inductive approaches are usually accompanied, or directly followed by, attempts to cover the new set of phenomena under a broader theoretical or conceptual umbrella; that is, by modifying some available nominal definition of political participation.

A nominal definition is an agreement about the use of a term or word (definiendum) by referring to an already known notion or known terms (definiens). Nominal definitions contain no empirical information but are meant to avoid misunderstandings and to make discussions easier. Such a definition cannot be true or false, but can turn out to be, for instance, useful or useless. For example, in 1979 Kaase and Marsh (1979b, 169) found that a number of citizens in The Netherlands, Britain, the US, Germany, and Austria had been engaged in unconventional participatory activities such as signing petitions and participating in demonstrations. With these protest actions becoming widely popular in at least the five societies they explored, it would have been unthinkable to retain a working definition of political participation that would not cover them. Their expanded definition of political participation as "all voluntary activities by individual citizens intended to influence either directly or indirectly political choices at various levels of the political system" (Kaase and Marsh 1979a, 42) allowed them to study these new forms of participation without excluding conventional modes of behavior. More importantly, this conceptual modification enabled them to explore the profound democratic changes taking place in many countries systematically by focusing on the newly arising unconventional forms of political participation. For participation research relying on a nominal definition, therefore, the answer to the question how to deal with the continuous rise of new forms of participation is simple: if the world changes, then you have to update your terms accordingly.

Obviously, no arguments are needed to underline the importance of clear, unambiguous, and complete definitions of terms in any discussion deserving its name. Yet it can be questioned whether the nominal approach, i.e. coming up with a sentence-long, carefully trimmed phrase, solves the challenges of dealing with continuous expansions of the repertoire of political participation. First, disagreement about the meaning of terms already starts at a rather basic level. Whereas, for instance, Milbrath and Goel (1977, 2) included "support government and politics" in their previously cited definition (in Section 3.2) of politics as "those actions of private citizens by which they seek to influence or to support government and politics", most authors since seem to agree with Verba and Nie (1972) that "support participation" should be excluded. Instead of avoiding misunderstandings, then, the practice of revising or modifying nominal definitions seems, in practice, to be hardly any different from inductive approaches.

An example of how such an approach can have consequences for the development of a concept is provided by Norris, who in the early 2000s noted that the classic definition of political participation cited earlier no longer covered all activities considered relevant. Consequently, she expanded the definition and proposed that political participation can be thought of as "any dimensions of activity that are either designed directly to influence government agencies and the policy process, or indirectly to impact civil society, or which attempt to alter systematic patterns of social behavior" (Norris 2001, 16). This definition clearly makes an important step in opening up to acts that are not strictly confined to the realm of government and politics. Yet it expands the definition considerably by introducing "systematic patterns of social behaviour"—a term that may be interpreted in any number of ways, including a large number of social and political behaviors, some of which have absolutely nothing to do with politics. Returning a "good morning" to the porter of your institute who always wishes you a nice day is a "systematic pattern of social behaviour", but it is hard to imagine how it could be relevant for the study of political participation. Modifying nominal definitions usually means climbing to a higher rung on the "Ladder of Abstraction" (Sartori 1970) and implies the introduction of more abstract terms. On this newly achieved level, the price we have to pay for covering a larger set of phenomena is that our selection criteria become less specific—as Norris's definition clearly shows. By climbing the "Ladder", we end up with a "concept of everything"; that is, with a definition of participation that does not provide a demarcation between political participation on the one hand, and other specimen of human behavior on the other.

As with the inductive strategy, depending on nominal definitions means that with each newly arising form of political participation our definition has to be expanded accordingly (the story behind Norris's definition is, again, a good example). This leaves a number of available definitions floating around, each of whom is "correct" at a specific moment in time, for a specific group of scholars, or for research that has a more limited or a broader scope. Obviously, this development makes the entire effort to arrive at a common understanding about the expansion of participation even more troublesome.

3.3.3 Limiting Scope and Sphere

Confronted with the endless expansions of the forms of political participation and the accompanying definitional modifications, several authors tried to deal with these complications by taking a different road: defining non-political activities instead of political ones. Once again, Verba and Nie (1972, 2–3) confronted these problems in a pragmatic way and proposed to exclude from our understanding of political participation the following four phenomena:

1. Ceremonial or support participation.
2. Attitudes.
3. Participation in schools, family, job, voluntary associations.
4. Only "legal and legitimate" modes are considered, excluding most tactics of political protest.

The first two points reinforce the depiction of political participation as activities determined by citizens and can be easily accepted to limit the concept of participation. The criteria to limit participation mentioned under the very last point have been dropped from most participation studies—at least since the early 1980s—as being too much focused on status-quo-oriented behavior (Barnes et al. 1979). This leaves us with the suggestion to exclude activities in "schools, family, jobs, voluntary associations etcetera" from the definition of political participation. In a similar way, Parry, Moyser, and Day (1992, 16) explicitly indicated that their conceptualization of political participation does not incorporate the following:

1. Behavior not aimed at influencing public representatives (like going to an office to receive welfare benefits).
2. Participation in the workplace.
3. Showing interest in politics.
4. Displaying attitudes to support the functioning of democracy.
5. Readiness or willingness to take action.

The last three points are attitudes towards politics and should be dismissed on the basis of the criterion that participation refers to activities. Verba and Nie (1972, 3) also mentioned the second point and excluded participation "in other spheres—family, school, job, voluntary associations" from the concept of political participation, although they do point out that theorists have often regarded them as training ground for participation. The first point of Parry and his colleagues, however, brings us to the core of the debate, by including an aspect that cannot possibly be excluded from the definition of participation. Apparently, political participation has to be aimed at "influencing public representatives"; that is, all activities of people are to be excluded if they are not aimed at some "public" group or actor of representative government. In their more recent study in the US, Verba, Schlozman, and Brady (1995, 39) stress this aspect again: Excluded from political participation are all activities in which the "target audience is not a public official". Although this aspect covers important forms of political participation, a restriction to these phenomena has been correctly depicted as "unduly limited" (Norris 2002, 192).

With the gradual dissolution of the lines of demarcation between various societal, social, and economic spheres, a straightforward exclusion of activities in the workplace, schools, family, and voluntary associations is even less convincing now than it was in the 1970s or 1980s. Activities in voluntary associations are part of the communitarian and (neo) Tocquevillean revivals of the early 1990s and are considered to be politically relevant by many authors (see, for instance Zukin et al. 2006), not only because of their socializing role as "schools of democracy", but also because of their direct consequences on political life more broadly. Furthermore, the political nature of activities in spheres such as the workplace is evident during labor conflicts when strikes against government policies are at stake (Pateman 1970). However, many less dramatic events—such as, for example, signature actions among colleagues—usually can be easily recognized as specimen of political participation since the main object is political, and "public representatives" are often among the main addressees of these actions. This line of argument can be used for activities in schools and families as well. As a result, by excluding specific areas or spheres—such as the workplace and schools—*a priori*, definitions of political participation do not become less ambiguous; instead they become confusing rather soon. Besides, these restrictions certainly do not make it easier to deal with continuous expansions of the repertoire of political participation with expressive, creative and lifestyle-oriented forms which, almost by definition, reject restrictions to specific areas, spheres, or contexts.

3.4 The Need for Conceptual Improvements

For many years, one of the most persistent arguments in the literature on the quality of democracy is that citizen engagement in politics is declining. A wave of scholarship has argued against this idea. Yes, engagement in politics is declining, but not in all kinds of politics.

Traditional forms of participation related to electoral politics may be suffering from plunging participation rates, but other, new forms of engagement are on the rise. When it comes to the emerging forms of participation, however, scholarship either seems to have stopped short in its effort to define them, or has sought salvation in increasingly abstract definitions.

In this chapter, we have argued that political participation has expanded beyond electoral, civic, and protest acts into activities that are often very difficult to recognize as being political or politically relevant. The expansion of forms of political participation received much attention in the literature which, in the interest of developing a common language in political science, has attempted to generate definitions for these expansions without excluding the more conventional activities. This has proved to be an extremely challenging task. Narrow definitions focusing on government and politics have been expanded into more encompassing ones that also cover non- and extra-institutionalized activities. These concepts have been further expanded with even bolder attempts to define participation more broadly, as, for instance, patterns of social behavior. Important although this strategy may be for opening up the field to forms of political participation that do not fit political scientists' normative requirements and valued definitions, such open approaches risk to end up with a "concept of everything". This introduces a new—and potentially even more serious—problem, leading to a dangerously inconsistent way of measuring and comparing participation. If we do not succeed in handling this challenge in a more satisfying way, the quality of our assessment of how citizens practice democratic politics may range from less accurate to downright wrong.

What these issues make clear is that a new, fresh approach of conceptualizing and measuring political participation is needed. One that does not refuse to embed new features of contemporary political engagement and, at the same time, does not neglect the foundational criteria for establishing the political nature of a participatory act. This approach should rely on both the narrow and expanded characteristics of extant definitions and enable scholars to study systematically different manifestations of the same phenomenon across different contexts and points in time, using a common vocabulary.

Notes

1. Not all studies find positive effects, however, with a panel study by Gil de Zúñiga, Molyneux, and Zheng (2014) finding that social-media use

for social interaction did not affect people's political participation, and an experimental study by Theocharis and Lowe (2014) showing that Facebook adoption had a clear negative effect on both civic and political participation.

2. For a recent discussion and some evidence, see Lilleker and Koc-Michalska (2017).

3. For example, of the rich battery tested by Gibson, Lusoli, and Ward (2005) (which itself built on Krueger's [2002] work), not a single item ever made it to any of the waves of the ESS or the WVS (although, as mentioned in the previous chapter, this is mainly because of the way questions are adopted in large-scale surveys and not because of the authors' selection of items). Similarly, none of the items used by the PEW center in the studies mentioned in Chapter 2 have been adopted by major cross-national surveys, and even important national surveys in the US, such as the American National Election Study, still do not include a questionnaire unit with such questions.

References

Barberá, Pablo, Ning Wang, Richard Bonneau, John T Jost, Jonathan Nagler, Joshua Tucker, and Sandra González-Bailón. 2015. "The Critical Periphery in the Growth of Social Protests." *PLoS ONE* 10 (11). journals.plos.org/plosone/article?id=10.1371/journal.pone.0143611.

Barnes, Samuel H, Max Kaase, Klaus R Allerbeck, Barbara G Farah, Felix Heunks, Ronald Inglehart, M Kent Jennings, Hans-Dieter Klingemann, Alan Marsh, and Leopold Rosenmayr. 1979. *Political Action: Mass Participation in Five Western Democracies*. Beverly Hills: Sage.

Bennett, Lance W. 2012. "The Personalization of Politics: Political Identity, Social Media, and Changing Patterns of Participation." *The ANNALS of the American Academy of Political and Social Science* 644 (1): 20–39.

Bennett, Lance W, and Alexandra Segerberg. 2013. *The Logic of Connective Action: Digital Media and the Personalization of Contentious Politics*. Cambridge: Cambridge University Press.

Biggs, Michael, and Kenneth T Andrews. 2015. "Protest Campaigns and Movement Success." *American Sociological Review* 80 (2): 416–43.

Boyle, Michael P, Mike Schmierbach, Cory L Armstrong, Jaeho Cho, Michael McCluskey, Douglas M McLeod, and Dhavan Shah. 2006. "Expressive Responses to News Stories about Extremist Groups: A Framing Experiment." *Journal of Communication* 56: 271–88.

Brady, Henry E. 1999. "Political Participation." In *Measures of Political Attitudes*, edited by John P Robinson, Phillip R Shaver, and Lawrence S Wrightsman, 737–801. San Diego: Academic Press.

Casas, Andreu, and Nora W Williams. 2016. "Images That Matter: Online Protests and the Mobilizing Role of Pictures." *112th Annual Meeting of the American Political Science Association*. Philadelphia.

Conge, Patrick J. 1988. "The Concept of Political Participation: Toward a Definition." *Comparative Politics* 20 (2): 241–9.

Conway, Margaret M. 1991. *Political Participation in the United States.* Washington, DC: CQ Press.

Earl, Jennifer. 2000. "Methods, Movements, and Outcomes: Methodological Difficulties in the Study of Extra-Movement Outcomes." *Research in Social Movements, Conflicts and Change* 22 (1): 3–25.

Fox, Stuart. 2013. "Is It Time to Update the Definition of Political Participation? Political Participation in Britain: The Decline and Revival of Civic Culture." *Parliamentary Affairs* 67 (2): 495–505.

Freelon, Deen, Charlton McIlwain, and Meredith Clark. 2016. "Quantifying the Power and Consequences of Social Media Protest." *New Media & Society.* http://journals.sagepub.com/doi/abs/10.1177/1461444816676646.

Gibson, Rachel, Weiner Lusoli, and Stephen Ward. 2005. "Online Participation in the UK: Testing a 'Contextualised' Model of Internet Effects." *The British Journal of Politics and International Relations* 7 (4): 561–83.

Gil De Zúñiga, Homero, Logan Molyneux, and Pei Zheng. 2014. "Social Media, Political Expression, and Political Participation: Panel Analysis of Lagged and Concurrent Relationships." *Journal of Communication* 64 (4): 612–34.

Hay, Colin. 2007. *Why We Hate Politics.* Cambridge: Polity Press.

Jungherr, Andreas, and Pascal Jürgens. 2014. "Through a Glass, Darkly: Tactical Support and Symbolic Association in Twitter Messages Commenting on Stuttgart 21." *Social Science Computer Review* 32 (1): 74–89.

Kaase, Max, and Alan Marsh. 1979a. "Political Action: A Theoretical Perspective." In *Political Action: Mass Participation in Five Western Democracies*, by Samuel H Barnes, Max Kaase, Klaus R Allerbeck, Barbara G Farah, Felix Heunks, Ronald Inglehart, M Kent Jennings, Hans-Dieter Klingemann, Alan Marsh, and Leopold Rosenmayr, 27–56. Beverly Hills: Sage.

———. 1979b. "Political Action Repertory: Changes over Time and a New Typology." In *Political Action: Mass Participation in Five Western Democracies*, by Samuel H Barnes, Max Kaase, Klaus R Allerbeck, Barbara G Farah, Felix Heunks, Ronald Inglehart, M Kent Jennings, Hans-Dieter Klingemann, Alan Marsh, and Leopold Rosenmayr, 137–66. Beverly Hills: Sage.

Kahne, Joseph, Nam-Jin Lee, and Jessica T Feezell. 2013. "The Civic and Political Significance of Online Participatory Cultures among Youth Transitioning to Adulthood." *Journal of Information Technology & Politics* 10 (1): 1–20.

Kam, Cindy D. 2012. "Risk Attitudes and Political Participation." *American Journal of Political Science* 56 (4): 817–36.

Karpf, David. 2010. "Online Political Mobilization from the Advocacy Group's Perspective: Looking beyond Clicktivism." *Policy & Internet* 2 (4): 7–41.

———. 2016. *Analytic Activism.* New York: Oxford University Press.

Kobayashi, Tetsuro, and Yu Ichifuji. 2015. "Tweets That Matter: Evidence from a Randomized Field Experiment in Japan." *Political Communication* 32 (4): 574–93.

Krueger, Brian. 2002. "Assessing the Impact of Internet Political Participation in the United States: A Resource Approach." *American Political Research* 30 (5): 476–98.

Lilleker, Darren G, and Karolina Koc-Michalska. 2017. "What Drives Political Participation? Motivations and Mobilization in a Digital Age." *Political Communication* 34 (1): 21–43.

MacKinnon, Rebecca. 2013. *Consent of the Networked: The Worldwide Struggle for Internet Freedom.* New York: Basic Books.

McCaughey, Martha, and Michael D Ayers. 2003. *Cyberactivism: Online Activism in Theory and Practice.* New York: Routledge.

Milbrath, Lester W, and Madan L Goel. 1977. *Political Participation: How and Why Do People Get Involved in Politics.* Chicago: Rand McNally.

Morozov, Evgeny. 2009. "The Brave New World of Slacktivism." *Foreign Policy Blogs.* foreignpolicy.com/2009/09/05/from-slacktivism-to-activism.

———. 2013. "The Limits of Technology in an Imperfect World." London. www.chathamhouse.org/sites/files/chathamhouse/public/Meetings/Meeting Transcripts/180313MorozovQA.pdf.

Norris, Pippa. 2001. "Count Every Voice: Democratic Participation Worldwide." www.pippanorris.com.

———. 2002. *Democratic Phoenix: Reinventing Political Activism.* Cambridge: Cambridge University Press.

Parry, Geraint, George Moyser, and Neil Day. 1992. *Political Participation and Democracy in Britain.* Cambridge: Cambridge University Press.

Pateman, Carole. 1970. *Participation and Democratic Theory.* Cambridge: Cambridge University Press.

Rojas, Hernando, and Eulalia Puig-I-Abril. 2009. "Mobilizers Mobilized: Information, Expression, Mobilization and Participation in the Digital Age." *Journal of Computer-Mediated Communication* 14 (4): 902–27.

Sajuria, Javier, Jennifer vanHeerde-Hudson, David Hudson, Niheer Dasandi, and Yannis Theocharis. 2015. "Tweeting Alone? An Analysis of Bridging and Bonding Social Capital in Online Networks." *American Politics Research* 43 (4): 708–38.

Sartori, Giovanni. 1970. "Concept Misformation in Comparative Politics." *American Political Science Review* 64 (4): 1033–53.

Schlozman, Kay Lehman, Sidney Verba, and Henry E Brady. 2012. *The Unheavenly Chorus: Unequal Political Voice and the Broken Promise of American Democracy.* Princeton: Princeton University Press.

Theocharis, Yannis. 2015. "The Conceptualization of Digitally Networked Participation." *Social Media + Society* 1 (2): 1–14.

Theocharis, Yannis, and Will Lowe. 2014. "Does Facebook Increase Political Participation? Evidence from a Field Experiment." *Information, Communication & Society* 19 (10): 1465–86.

Time. 2016. "The Lasting Effects of Occupy Wall Street, Five Years Later." *Time,* September. http://time.com/money/4495707/occupy-wall-street-anniversary-effects/.

Tufekci, Zeynep. 2012. "#Kony2012, Understanding Networked Symbolic Action & Why Slacktivism Is Conceptually Misleading." *Technosociology, Our Tools, Ourselves.* technosociology.org/?p=904.

————. 2014. "What Happens to #Ferguson Affects Ferguson: Net Neutrality, Algorithmic Filtering and Ferguson." *Medium.com*. https://medium.com/message/ferguson-is-also-a-net-neutrality-issue-6d2f3db51eb0.

van Deth, Jan W. 2001. "Studying Political Participation: Towards a Theory of Everything?" *Joint Sessions of Workshops of the European Consortium for Political Research*. Grenoble.

————. 2014. "A Conceptual Map of Political Participation." *Acta Politica* 49 (3): 349–67.

Verba, Sidney, and Norman H Nie. 1972. *Participation in America: Political Democracy and Social Equality*. Chicago: University of Chicago Press.

Verba, Sidney, Kay Lehman Schlozman, and Henry E Brady. 1995. *Voice and Equality: Civic Voluntarism in American Politics*. Cambridge: Harvard University Press.

Vissers, Sara, and Dietlind Stolle. 2014. "The Internet and New Modes of Political Participation: Online versus Offline Participation." *Information, Communication & Society* 17 (8): 937–55.

Zuckerman, Ethan. 2014. "New Media, New Civics?" *Policy & Internet* 6 (2): 151–68.

Zukin, Cliff, Scott Keeter, Molly Andolina, Krista Jenkins, and Michael X Delli Carpini. 2006. *A New Engagement? Political Participation, Civic Life, and the Changing American Citizen*. Oxford: Oxford University Press.

4 Conceptualizing Political Participation

> Traditional theoretical and conceptual frameworks derived from the literature of the 1960s and 1970s, and even what we mean by "political participation," need to be revised and updated to take account of how opportunities for civic engagement have evolved and diversified over the years.
>
> (Norris 2002, 188)

4.1 The Need for a Systematic Approach

The very diverse examples of the ways in which people participate nowadays that we have so far presented may suggest that, for all their novelty and creativity, these forms of participation hardly fit—or sometimes do not fit at all—with concepts underpinning our common understanding of what it means to participate in politics. Dealing with the expansion of the repertoire, scholars have tried to redefine participation, increasingly abandoning narrowly focused concepts, in favor of more "open" concepts that include all kinds of behavior. Although the merits and benefits of adopting more open definitions of political participation are clear, such definitions stretch the concept to include an infinite number of everyday acts, and thus risk defeating the purpose of providing a conceptualization in the first place. As we have shown in Chapter 3, available approaches for integrating into the repertoire of political participation forms that currently do not fit within accepted definitions, suffer from various problems. The most important problem is that scholars are prevented from systematically studying different manifestations of the same phenomenon across different contexts, using a common vocabulary. As the following quote by Norris shows, this problem has been recognized since the early 2000s, but little has been done since towards its solution:

Political participation is evolving and diversifying in terms of the *who* (the *agencies* or collective organizations), *what* (the *repertoire* of actions commonly used for political expression), and *where* (the *targets* that participants seek to influence). Admittedly, it is difficult to substantiate this argument with the limited empirical evidence available.

(2002, 4 italics in original)

A more systematic approach should enable scholars: (1) to use a set of commonly accepted criteria to decide whether a phenomenon can be defined as a form of political participation, (2) to discern whether it is a new mode of participation or whether it is a different manifestation of an existing mode, (3) to develop measures that can be used consistently in studies across different contexts, and which (4) can be used to estimate whether the prevalence of the phenomenon makes it worthy of further investigation. Applying such a systematic method enables scholars to assess the quality of democracy based on valid information on the repertoire of participation consisting of commonly accepted forms of participation as well as constantly created novel activities.

In this chapter, we propose a systematic method for conceptualizing political participation. This approach builds on our previous work (van Deth 2014; Theocharis 2015), and relies predominantly on the map presented by van Deth (2016, 2014), using fundamental definitional criteria included in all available conceptualizations of political participation as the building blocks of a rules-based system for classifying acts as political participation. The major advantage of this approach is that it is open to any phenomenon that has been (or will be) included in the repertoire of participation—be it voting, demonstrating, blogging, building a model city or dropping a seed-bomb in your neighborhood. Moreover, the approach very precisely specifies which criteria have to be fulfilled to depict a phenomenon as a form of political participation—or perhaps more importantly, to understand which properties the act under scrutiny lacks in order to qualify as one.

4.2 The Conceptual Map of Political Participation

Problems with the conceptualization of political participation are usually dealt with by inductive strategies, by modifying nominal definitions, or by limiting the objects under study (see Chapter 3). The conceptual map of political participation represents a more pragmatic approach by systematically identifying the indispensable requirements for some phenomena to be recognized as specimens of political participation. In other words, the initial question "what is political participation" is converted into a practical task: How do you recognize a mode of participation if you see one?

The fresh approach for identifying and defining an act as political participation is based on the development of an *operational definition* of political participation, specifying the exact properties that are required to determine its existence.[1] A useful point of departure for understanding the logic behind the map's operation is Hempel's (1965) seminal work on taxonomies and classifications, in which he pointed out to two general requirements for operational definitions. First, an operational definition should provide "objective criteria by means of which any scientific investigator can decide, for any particular case, whether the term does or does not apply" (Hempel 1965, 141; see also Sartori 1970, 1045). By pointing to, for instance, voluntariness or government directedness in definitions of political participation, such criteria are already widely used in exactly this way. What is needed for more specific distinctions between different phenomena is a systematically developed *set of decision rules* to answer the question whether we can depict a specific phenomenon as political participation. Second, Hempel not only stated that these decision rules have to be unambiguous; he stressed that they have to be efficient by placing them in a hierarchical order. In a hierarchically ordered classification, each subgroup is "defined by the specification of necessary and sufficient conditions of membership" (Hempel 1965, 138). Following this recommendation, for political participation we need to develop a *minimal definition* of the concept before more complex variants are considered.[2] The advantage of this smallest set of decision rules is that we can deal with unproblematic cases easily: Because no sophisticated arguments are required to recognize voting or contacting a politician as specimens of political participation, we should focus on properties which might bring, for example, community work, boycotting products, and changing ones' profile picture on Facebook under the same label.

Suppose we encounter a new phenomenon for which we want to know whether the term political participation does or does not apply. This question can be answered for any phenomenon by going through various steps, each representing a decision rule in a hierarchical scheme. Figure 4.1 presents an overview of the eight decision rules proposed, each of which can be answered by confirming or rejecting the availability of a property with "yes" or "no", respectively. If the

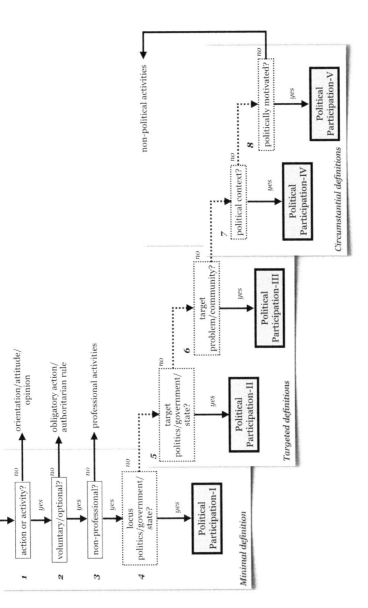

Figure 4.1 The conceptual map of political participation

availability of a certain property is there, then we move on to the next property of the phenomenon—if a property is not found, the phenomenon under consideration is not a specimen of political participation as defined by the confirmed properties so far. In this last case, further properties are required. In the following, we present the eight rules to define political participation and apply them to discern a typology of five major modes of political participation.

Rule 1: Is It an Activity or Action?

Nominal definitions of participation all start with references to behavioral aspects; participation requires an activity or action (Verba and Nie 1972; Parry, Moyser, and Day 1992). Being interested in politics or watching newscasts is not sufficient. Only few authors have challenged this behavioral aspect of participation and have broaden the scope to "latent forms of political participation" (Ekman and Amnå 2012, 287—see also Conway's definition in Section 3.2 [p. 46]). To secure the analytical distinction between effects and attitudinal determinants of participation, the almost unanimous restriction to participation-as-an-activity is followed here. Yet stressing the behavioral nature of any phenomenon eventually to be labeled as a specimen of political participation does not avoid all ambiguities. Specific abstentions of activities— for instance boycotting certain products, staying away from the ballot box, refusing to donate money—are, strictly speaking, not instances of activities or actions. Nonetheless, many people "regard their own decision not to participate in formal politics as itself a highly political act" (Hay 2007, 26). Only in case abstentions are used in similar ways as activities, should these "activities" also be treated as a satisfactory fulfillment of this first rule's requirement. For example, only refusing to buy truly obtainable products, staying at home on an actual election day, or refusing to pay charges are accepted as specimens of relevant "activities" here. Although these specifications are difficult to capture in empirical research—indeed such a motivation remains literally invisible in surveys—using additional evidence and carefully phrased questions can deal with such nuances.

Rule 2: Is the Activity Voluntary?

In a democracy, political participation should not be a consequence of force, pressure, or threats, but be optional and based on free will. Because examining a person's free will is highly

problematic in empirical research, a negative formulation empha-
sizing the absence of observable coercion—including unreason-
ably high costs—seems to be more practical. Examples of such
coercions are, first of all, legal obligations or mandatory tasks, but
also economic or social extortions. However, paying taxes, sitting
in a traffic jam, or appearing in court are all examples of invol-
untary acts with (potentially) political consequences that should
be excluded from the concept of political participation. Notice
that this rule does not exclude "compulsory voting" from the concept of political participation. Contrary to what the term suggests,
actually casting a vote cannot be mandatory in any system guar-
anteeing secret elections (a main feature of democracy). In some
countries citizens are obliged to report to the polling station on
election day, but no democracy has ever enforced actual voting.

Rule 3: Is the Activity Conducted by Non-professionals?

Most definitions of political participation explicitly refer to "citizens" in order to differentiate the relevant behavior from the
activities of politicians, civil servants, office-bearers, public offi-
cers, journalists, and professional delegates, advisors, appoin-
tees, lobbyists, and the like. Essential as the accomplishments of
these functionaries and officials might be for the political system,
using the concept of political participation in those instances
would stretch the range of relevant behavior to cover conceptually and functionally very different phenomena. The same applies
to commercial activities. Therefore, the term "citizen" is explicitly
incorporated into many definitions of political participation to
underline the non-professional, nonpaid, amateur nature of activities (Stoker 2006). Some authors use the term "citizen participation" to avoid any misunderstanding (Callahan 2007).

Rule 4: Is the Activity Located in the Sphere of Government/State/Politics?

The adjective "political" is a crucial part of any conceptualization
of political participation. Circular definitions are widely available
and easy recognizable by the inclusion of terms such as "politics,"
"political system," "public policy," or "policy process" in the expli-
cans. Somewhat more informative are references to "government",
"government agencies", or "public representatives and officials".
Because "politics", "government", or "democracy" are essentially
contested concepts (Gallie 1956), no conceptualization of political

participation can avoid the question whether the activities considered are located in the political sector of society; that is, the sector directed by government under the jurisdiction of state power. Since we want to arrive at a minimal definition of political participation first, this rule should be based on the most straightforward condition available. The institutional architecture of the political system ("polity") seems to fulfill this requirement.

These four decision rules already suffice to reach *a minimal definition* of political participation. By focusing on the locus (or arena) of participation—rather than on outcomes, legality, collective versus individual nature, intentions, etc.—as the defining characteristic, all nonprofessional, voluntary activities located in the sphere of government/state/politics are specimens of political participation; labeled here as **Political Participation-I.**[3] This mode of participation includes activities such as casting a vote for the German general election or for a referendum in Switzerland, starting or signing an online petition at petition.parliament.uk to be taken into consideration by the British parliament, contributing to the Democratic Party or working for Hilary Clinton's campaign in the US presidential election, or being active in New York City Council's participatory budgeting. Frequently used terms for activities meeting the four requirements of the minimal definition are "conventional" (Stolle, Hooghe, and Micheletti 2005, 249), "institutionalized" (Hooghe and Quintelier 2014, 214), or "elite-directed" (Inglehart, 1977, 5) modes of political participation.

Yet, it is clear that a minimal definition of participation is not sufficient to cover all citizens' political activities. Although early overviews simply excluded "the politics of nongovernmental organizations" and "political demonstrations" from the object of study (Milbrath 1965, 1, 18), in any vibrant democracy, forms of political participation exist outside the regular government/state/politics sphere, and usually explicitly challenge the status quo. Hay (2007, 75) points to such forms that "take place outside of the governmental arena, yet respond to concerns that are formally recognized politically and on which there may well be active legislative or diplomatic agendas". Therefore, in case the activity concerned is not located in the sphere of government/state/politics (Rule 4), a further rule is required to cover those activities.

Rule 5: Is the Activity Targeted at the Sphere of Government/State/Politics?

Activities that are not located in the government/state/politics arena can be considered as modes of political participation if they are *targeted* at that sphere. Many of these modes are used to attract public attention to issues that either have not been perceived as problematic or have not been recognized as problems requiring governmental/state involvement so far. Certainly, in the initial stage of their application these modes intend to challenge the conventional understanding of the scope and nature of politics, and the domain of government in a society. Labels such as "contentious politics" (Tilly and Tarrow 2006) or "elite-challenging politics" (Inglehart 1990, 338) underline the conflictual nature of these activities. Although the actions usually aim at expanding the understanding of politics and government, they are also used to limit state intervention (for instance when workers block streets to stop the regulation of labor conditions).

If the objectives of the activities indeed include politics or the addressees are located in government or the state, then this is a second main type of political participation (**Political Participation-II**). The decisive point is that this feature refers to the targets of the activities considered, and not to the aims or intentions of activists. Targeted political activities are covered by, for example, the Cross-National Time-Series Data Archive definition of "peaceful demonstrations" as "any peaceful gathering of more than 100 people for the primary purpose of displaying or voicing their opposition to government policies or authorities" (Banks 2009, as cited by Teorell 2010, 168). This definition shows clearly how the targets of the activities can be depicted without relying on the goals or intentions of the people involved. It is important to note here that activities which are now frequently carried out through social-media platforms such as Facebook and Twitter—and are often derided due to their low costs—conform fully to this type of political participation from a conceptual point of view. For example, addressing a politician on Twitter using her @handle—a direct and public act that often receives feedback—is an activity that does not take place *within* the formal locus of politics (Twitter is a commercial social-media platform in which a politician may or may not have a profile), yet it is clearly and unambiguously targeted towards a politician who has made available to citizens this channel of direct communication.

Rule 6: Is the Activity Aimed at Solving Collective or Community Problems?

Government and state agencies are not the only targets of political activities, and scholars of participation have stressed the relevance of communal activities and voluntary associations frequently

(Verba, Nie, and Kim 1978; Verba, Schlozman, and Brady 1995; Verba and Nie 1972). Discussions about political participation and civic engagement indicate that participation seems to be increasingly focused "on problem solving and helping others" (Zukin et al. 2006, 7). This conceptualization is too broad to produce a useful definition of political participation. Yet, problem solving or helping others certainly can be accepted as modes of political participation if clearly private or non-public activities are excluded. To attain the adjective "political" for problem solving and helping others, these activities should be aimed at shared problems which existing policies do not address, and which usually, but not necessarily, means that community problems are at the center. Hay (2007, 75) brings this conceptualization to the point: "actions might be deemed political only in so far as they either arise out of situations of collective choice or are likely to have collective consequences, at whatever point these consequences arise". This solution seems more pragmatic than opening the already mentioned debate on the essentially contested nature of concepts such as "politics", "government", or "democracy" once again. To deny the adjective "political" to attempts to solve collective or community problems would imply a restriction to government- and state-centered definitions of political participation, and—what is much more problematic—to an exclusion of activities by people who explicitly reject some borderline between "politics" and "society". For that reason, these activities are distinguished from other modes of participation but, taking into consideration that the recognition that the lines between political and civic engagement are blurred, they are not eliminated from the broader conceptualization of political participation.

Non-professional, voluntary activities that are not located in, or targeted at, the sphere of government/state/politics can be considered as modes of political participation if they are aimed at solving collective or community problems. Notice that it is the character of the problem dealt with that has to be collective or shared, not the organizational aspects of the activities undertaken. Especially newer forms of participation are labeled as "individualized collective action" to underline this distinction (Micheletti 2003, 28). If this last condition is met, a second variant of a targeted definition of political participation is arrived at, now aimed at solving collective or community problems (**Political Participation-III**). Examples of activities belonging to this category are citizens' initiatives to combat drug abuse in the community, participation in neighborhood committees, sharing a link about a recent violent incident perpetrated by the local police force on the Facebook page of Communities United Against Police Brutality (CUAPB), or directly tweeting a message against police brutality in your state to some police department's Twitter account. As with the government/politics/state-targeted definition, no references to aims or intentions of participants have to be considered for this second variant. Especially authors working in the field of civil society and social capital favor the depiction of activities aimed at solving collective or community problems as modes of political participation. Macedo and his collaborators (2005, 6, italics in original), for example, define "civic engagement" as *"any activity, individual or collective, devoted to influencing the collective life of the polity"*—a rather broad definition that perfectly matches the two types of targeted definitions of political participation (**Political Participation-II and -III**).

Rule 7: Is the Activity Placed in a Political Context?

The expansion of the minimum definition with targeted definitions, however, does not exhaust the repertoire of citizens' political activities in a democracy. Especially young people—who research has shown to be disappointed and disengaged with traditional channels of participation, but who are not unexcited, uninterested, or not opinionated about politics (Cammaerts et al. 2014)—are increasingly keener on personalizing their engagement in politics (Bennett 2012). This type of engagement is often not limited to young people and does not meet any of the three conditions for previous definitions of political participation (Rules 4, 5, and 6). In such cases, we are apparently dealing with some voluntary, non-professional activity that is neither located in, nor targeted at, government/state/politics or at solving community problems—but is used to express ethical or moral concerns and is usually geared towards raising awareness. Many forms of digitally networked participation which are "carried out by individual citizens with the intent to display their own mobilization and activate their social networks in order to raise awareness about, or exert social and political pressures for the solution of, a social or political problem" (Theocharis 2015, 6) are such activities. Many newer, "creative", "expressive", "personalized", and "individualized" modes of participation also seem to fit this category (Rojas and Puig-I-Abril 2009; Micheletti and Stolle 2010; Bennett 2012). An important aspect of these newer forms of political participation is that they typically "refer not to 'politics' as a noun, but to the 'political' as an adjective, describing the motivations of actors wherever such motivations might be displayed" (Hay 2007, 63). The depiction of political participation as "responsibility taking" (Stolle and Micheletti 2013, 34–35) by individual citizens, or as "doing it for fun, but also because you find it necessary" (Bang 2005, 169), underlines the ethical and moral connotations attached to these new forms.

An initial way to find out whether an apparently non-political activity is used for political purposes is to consider the specific context of the activity (Theocharis 2015). For instance, encamping or staging a play are, as such, not political activities, but they can easily become so if they are done at the gates of Downing Street, or in front of the European Central Bank. Similarly, a tweet that includes an image with several people throwing their hands in the air and is tagged with #Dontshoot, or a tweet including an image with two different photos tagged with #IfTheyGunnedMeDown, may both look suspiciously like acts of pure self-expression (Figure 4.2, images left and right respectively). Yet, in both cases, the hashtags used provide direct information about the context, which is unambiguously political and, in many cases, is embedded into a highly coordinated effort by a relevant activist/ advocacy organization (Karpf 2010). In the first photo, for example, the individuals aren't raising their hands in the air for a simple group photo, but to protest police violence, as is evident from the relevant hashtag that emerged in response to the shooting of Michael Brown (Time 2014). In the second image, the user juxtaposes two different images of himself, protesting the way in which the media choose to depict young black men (Süddeutsche Zeitung 2014).

By using contextual information (Rule 7), a nuanced way becomes available to deal with non-political activities. Circumstantial evidence required can be derived from the surrounding, environment, background, or setting of these non-political activities—not from the aims or intentions of the participants (see Rule 8), although these participants might underline the political nature of their activities by contributing to the context of their actions. A march of people meticulously dressed up as money-eating zombies could easily be confused with a carnival-related event, but probably not if it's taking place outside the New York stock exchange during the height of the global financial crisis. Especially for internet-based activities, the circumstances are often easily identifiable through hashtags or other such cues included

Figure 4.2 Screenshots of images posted on Twitter, using the #Dontshoot and #IfTheyGunnedMeDown hashtags

Source and credit for left image: Twitter user @*Anni_Wol*; source and credit for right image: Twitter user @DevGriffin618.

in the act (Theocharis 2015). For example, whereas posting political commentary on a community organization's Facebook page is a specimen of **Political Participation-III** (due to the fact that it targets a community), posting a political commentary *on one's own* Facebook or Twitter page for others to see, or encouraging others to take action on a political or social issue on one's own Facebook or Twitter page, are forms of political participation that belong to a different category, because the political context is made immediately available by the author, leaving no doubt about the issue to which the act is tied to (and also potentially revealing the individual's motivation). What is often insufficiently considered is that, from the moment the person decides to engage in this manner on his or her personal page, the act assumes a (usually irreversible) public character, as it becomes visible to one's social circle. It is thus important to note that, by acquiring a public character, some digitally networked acts, also acquire far higher *costs*, especially when posting one's opinion results in heated arguments and frustration.

Non-professional, voluntary activities that are not located in, or targeted at, the sphere of government/state/politics can be considered as modes of political participation if contextual evidence underlines the political nature of these activities. In this way, we arrive at a first variant of a circumstantial definition: **Political Participation-IV**.

Rule 8: Is the Activity Used to Express Political Aims and Intentions?

A final way to trace possible political characteristics in non-political activities is to rely on explicit expressions of the person involved: buying a brand of coffee is, as such, not a political activity. However, this can easily become a political activity if the shopper explicitly expresses his intention that this purchase should be understood as an utterance against import regulations. Similarly, as Penney's (2015, 63–64) qualitative research on the intentions of people who change/integrate their Facebook profile picture into a symbol of a political campaign (e.g. the equal sign in support of same-sex marriage) has shown, this seemingly non-political act is often used with the intention of creating visibility for supporters, raising awareness, and strengthening collective identity of around the purpose of the campaign. Many definitions of political participation include explicit references to goals or intentions and embrace references to activities that "intend" or are "aimed at" influencing government policies or the selection of its personnel. Undoubtedly, political participation is usually initiated and guided by the wish to have some impact on existing arrangements (Schlozman, Verba, and Brady 2012; Milbrath 1965) but, as research suggests, motivations play a complex role in influencing someone's decision to participate (be that online or offline), and it is difficult to distinguish between intrinsic and extrinsic motivations (Ryan and Deci 2000; Lilleker and Koc-Michalska 2017). The question, therefore, is not whether teleological aspects can or should be included in conceptualizations of political participation after we have dealt with minimal, targeted, and contextual definitions. The question is how to include such aspects in our understanding of political participation consistently. After applying the first seven rules, no general answer to this question is required because the political relevance of casting a vote or posting on your community's Facebook group is evident without looking at the motivations behind these activities. The introduction of subjective aspects is, therefore, only required when we reach non-political activities at the endpoint of our set of decision-making rules.

Any activity that fulfills the first three rules—activity, voluntariness, non-professional—but is not located in the political arena, is not aimed at either political actors or community problems, and is not placed in a political context, can be depicted as a form of political participation if the activity is used to express political aims and intentions by the participants. But what, one may ask, would such an activity look like? The examples can probably stretch as far as individuals' imaginations. In order to make clear what we have in mind, we use the case of MIT student Jonah Peretti, as described by him in an article in *The Nation*:

> Nike's website allows visitors to create custom shoes bearing a word or slogan—a service Nike trumpets as being about freedom to choose and freedom to express who you are. Confronted with Nike's celebration of freedom and their statement that if you want it done right, build it yourself, I could not help but think of the people in crowded factories in Asia and South America who actually build Nike shoes. As a challenge to Nike, I ordered a pair of shoes custom-ized with the word "sweatshop." Nike rejected my request, marking the beginning of a correspondence between me and the company [. . .]. None of Nike's messages addressed the company's legendary labor abuses, and their avoidance of the issue created an impression even worse than an admission of guilt. In mid-January I forwarded the whole e-mail correspondence to a dozen friends, and since that time it has raced around the Internet, reaching millions of people, even though I did not participate at all in its further proliferation. The e-mail began to spread widely thanks to a collection of strang-ers, scattered around the world, who took up my battle with Nike. Nike's adversary was an amorphous group of disgruntled consumers connected by a decentralized network of e-mail addresses.
>
> (2001)

Peretti's activities, which have been influential for scholars studying participation (McCaughey and Ayers 2003), are an apt example of an act of political participation (or, more specifically, political consumer-ism). His justification—"I could not help but think of the people in crowded factories in Asia and South America who actually build Nike shoes"—is required to understand his motives. Micheletti (2003, 14) stresses that "political consumerism is politics when people knowingly target market actors to express their opinions on justice, fairness, or noneconomic issues that concern personal and family well-being". Depending on the aims and intentions of the participants, applying Rule 8 results in a second variant of a circumstantial definition of political participation based on expressed intentions (**Political Participation-V**). This type covers all voluntary, non-political activities by citizens used to express their political aims and intentions, but which do not fit into one of the previous four types of participation.

With non-political activities used for political reasons, we have obviously reached the final borderline of our conceptual map of political participation. Notice, however, that intentions or aims of participants are only considered at this very last stage: Explicit expressions are only considered if none of the other potential features of participation is available. Obviously, these intentions and aims are usually highly interesting aspects of political phenomena, but we do not need them to depict most forms of political participation. Ockham's razor should be used whenever possible. By organizing the crucial criteria hierarchically (see the order of the five decision boxes with dotted borders in Figure 4.1), concluding whether a feature is available becomes increasingly complicated. Positively formulated, this means that phenomena such as casting a vote, contacting a politician, posting a political message, or organizing a budget forum can be identified as forms of political participation straightforwardly. Only after these relatively uncomplicated forms are dealt with more difficult criteria such as circumstantial evidence and motivations are considered.

Principally, there is no reason to restrict the application of Rule 8 to activities that could not be categorized under the minimal, targeted, or contextual definitions. Although the intentions and aims of the people involved are not necessary for defining the first four types of participation, that does not exclude teleological aspects for further refinements of these concepts (van Deth 2014). Following the distinctions proposed by Hay (2007), each type of political participation can be divided into "political" or "non-political" activities depending on whether the activists are primarily motivated by political or by non-political aims or intentions, respectively. Downs famously excluded casting a vote for party B instead of the preferred party A from his concept of "rational behavior" if for some voter "preventing his wife's tantrums is more important to him than having A win instead of B" (Downs 1957, 7). By using this argument, for instance, for modes of participation covered by the minimal definition, we arrive at the two variants of voting by Downsian citizens: a politically motivated form for those who base their vote for Party A on their political preferences, and a non-political form for those who prefer Party A, but vote for B to avoid further conflicts at home. Although these last forms of non-political participation provide an interesting case for the study of participation and democracy (van Deth 2014), they do not establish a distinct variant of political participation and are therefore not included in Figure 4.1.

4.3 Applying the Map to Conceptualize Participation

The advantages of the map can be illustrated by applying the decision rules to several phenomena. Table 4.1 provides an overview of how researchers can decide, first, whether or not the phenomena to be studied are to be considered a form of political participation and, second, to specify the criteria for this decision based on the application of the eight hierarchically organized rules. For illustrative purposes, a number of participatory activities are examined, ranging from the rather conventional ones, such as voting and protesting, to more exotic, such as spreading seedbombs, tagging photos on Instagram, or sharing links about political issues on Facebook. For each of these chosen phenomena we start with Rule 1—is it an act or activity?—and move on with the next questions until we reach an endpoint. In case we are dealing with a form of political participation, this endpoint will be one of the five modes of participation (**Participation-I** to **-V**) defined by the last positive answer provided. Yet in order to arrive at one of these endpoints it is clear that the first three rules (activity, voluntariness, non-professionalism) all have to be confirmed. If none of the Rules from 5 to 8 applies, we are obviously dealing with a non-political activity. By filtering out relevant and irrelevant features of the objects we study, the application of the map results in unambiguous and specific operational definitions which can be summarized by rows of Xs in Table 4.1: the longer a row is, the more features have to be taken into account to define the phenomenon.

As can be seen, the map is able to filter out non-political activities such as buying a specific brand of coffee. In a similar way, "liking" a post on Facebook fails to be considered as political participation already from the first rule, as it doesn't qualify as an activity. "Liking" something is an expression of preference or an attitude, and although it has the potential to lead to more meaningful engagement (usually in a chain of events or through strength in numbers), it does not even sufficiently convey the individual's intentions (Theocharis 2015, 8). On the other hand, the highly debated (New Statesman 2015) and criticized act of changing one's profile picture in solidarity with the

Table 4.1 Classification examples based on the conceptual map of participation

Example/phenomenon	Rule								Classification
	1 activity?	2 voluntary?	3 non-professional?	4 locus: pol/gov/state?	5 target: pol/gov(state)?	6 target: probl/comm?	7 political context?	8 politically motivated?	
Casting a vote	x	x	x	x	→				Political Participation-I (minimal definition)
Addressing a politician on Twitter using @handle	x	x	x	-	x	→			Political Participation-II (targeted definition: pol/gov/state)
Participating in a demonstration against import regulations	x	x	x	-	x	→			Political Participation-II (targeted definition: pol/gov/state)
Volunteering in a community effort to combat drug abuse	x	x	x	-	-	x	→		Political Participation-III (targeted definition: probl/community)
Posting a photo on Instagram with your hands raised to support #BlackLivesMatters	x	x	x	-	-	-	x	→	Political Participation-IV (circumstantial definition: context)

(Continued)

Table 4.1 (Continued)

Activity							Category
Spreading seedbombs to let flowers grow in a no-public-access abandoned site in your neighbourhood	x	x	-	-	x	↑	Political Participation-III (targeted definition: probl/community)
Changing your profile picture on Facebook into a flag, in solidarity with the victims of a terrorist attack	x	x	-	-	-	-	Non-political activity
Forwarding an email about Nike's refusal to use the phrase "sweatshop"	x	x	-	-	-	x	Political Participation-V (circumstantial definition: motivation)
Buying a specific brand of coffee	x	x	-	-	-	-	Non-political activity
Sharing a link about the government's legalisation of same-sex marriage on Facebook	x	x	-	-	x	↑	Political Participation-IV (circumstantial definition: context)
Liking a post of Facebook	-					⇒	(orientation/attitude/opinion)

victims of a terrorist attack, exploits the full filtering functions of the map. Contrary to "liking", changing one's profile picture into the flag of a country that suffered a terrorist attack is a highly visible act in the context of social media and resembles something that people want to publicly identify with. After being cleared off the locus of politics (Rule 4), this act is also filtered out from targeting the government (Rule 5) or a community problem (Rule 6), as there are no specific targets being addressed. Although terrorism certainly is a political issue, a contextual definition (Rule 7) does not cover the act as political participation because changing's one's profile picture is not meant to be about the issue of terrorism *per se*, but rather about the mourning of a nation for the victims of the terrorist attack. Similarly, the intention (Rule 8) usually is to self-declare one's solidarity with fellow human beings—although it also may simply be an effort to appear more sympathetic to others (New Statesman 2015). This act, therefore, fails the five crucial, rule-based criteria of the map, ending up as a non-political activity.

In Table 4.1 the exemplary phenomena all are filtered out unambiguously to reach a single endpoint of the map. Yet frequently several criteria can be satisfied to classify some activity; that is, a "chief implication of the use of the conceptual map to identify a specific phenomenon as a type of political participation is that the same phenomena do not always end up in the same category" (van Deth 2014, 360). For instance, seedbombs might be thrown by somebody who is strongly motivated by the desire to have flowers grown in a long-abandoned plot, the access to which has been blocked—which would depict throwing seedbombs as **Political Participation-V** and **-II**, respectively, and not as **-III** as indicated in Table 4.1. By using the hierarchical nature of the map, these ambiguities are easily avoided as long as it is clear what the main feature of the activity concerned is. Clarifying this last point might not always be easy, but brings us to the heart of the conceptual problems we are dealing with: Throwing a seedbomb could mean different things and these distinctions should not be hidden behind a general definition of participation. The example of changing one's profile picture on Facebook (or other social media) shows similar ambiguities that should be faced and not neglected. If one changes one's profile picture during the British referendum on Europe by attaching the "vote remain" logo, or a "vote for Hillary" logo in the case of US elections, then the map's criterion for a circumstantial definition of political participation (Rule 7) clearly is fulfilled. However, in some cases fulfilling the criterion for circumstantial definitions is not possible, as the cause is not always as identifiable or as current as, for example, the Brexit referendum or the US elections at the moment they occurred. Websites such as *ActionSprout* allow anyone to create a custom profile picture overlay for their cause in order to share it with their supporters. In such cases, when digitally networked participation is understood as an act carried out with the intent to display one's "own mobilization and activate their social networks in order to raise awareness about, or exert social and political pressures for the solution of, a social or political problem" (Theocharis 2015, 6), the criterion for political motivation (Rule 8) is satisfied and we end up with a motivational definition of political participation. The selection of one of these depictions to characterize the act of changing one's profile picture, therefore, depends on the feature that is considered to be the most important, salient, or relevant. Applying the map brings these considerations to foreground systematically.

4.4 Preventing an Endless Conceptual Expansion

Would you recognize a mode of political participation if you see one? The continuous expansion of the repertoire of political participation in many democracies in the last decades has made this question increasingly difficult to answer. These complications are evident when we deal with the rise of expressive and personalized forms of participation, especially when internet-based acts are used. As we showed in Chapter 3, neither deductive analyses nor the development of all-embracing nominal definitions have (so far) resulted in conceptual clarity. More importantly, although the rise of new forms of participation may require the inclusion of circumstantial evidence or aims and goals of participants, these requirements should not force us to expand our concepts and to make them unnecessarily complicated.

To deal with these challenges we developed a conceptual map of political participation consisting of a set of eight hierarchically ordered decision rules. This set offers—as Hempel (1965) suggested—"objective criteria" to decide whether the term political participation applies to some phenomenon. Applying the map developed here results in the depiction of five analytically unambiguous modes of political participation: a minimal definition based on the locus of the activities, two additional variants based on the target (politics/government/state or problems/community), and two based on circumstantial evidence (contextual and motivational). Together, the five variants of political participation cover the whole repertoire of political participation systematically without excluding any mode of political participation unknown yet. At the same time, the endless expansion of the modes of political participation in modern democracies does not result in an endless conceptual expansion.

Notes

1. The term "operational definition" is used here as defined by Hempel (1965) and does not refer to the common (behavioralist) practice to "operationalize" some previously defined theoretical concept.
2. Definitions are "minimal" if they "deliberatively focus on the smallest possible number of attributes that are still seen as producing a viable standard" (Collier and Levitsky 1997, 433).
3. This depiction follows the labels proposed by van Deth (2014; van Deth 2016).

References

Bang, Henrik P. 2005. "Among Everyday Makers and Expert Citizens." In *Remaking Governance: Peoples, Politics and the Public Sphere*, edited by Janet Newman, 159–78. Bristol: Policy Press.

Bennett, Lance W. 2012. "The Personalization of Politics: Political Identity, Social Media, and Changing Patterns of Participation." *The ANNALS of the American Academy of Political and Social Science* 644 (1): 20–39.

Callahan, Kathe. 2007. "Citizen Participation: Models and Methods." *International Journal of Public Administration* 30 (11). Routledge: 1179–96.

Cammaerts, Bart, Michael Bruter, Banaji Shakuntala, Sarah Harisson, and Nick Anstead. 2014. "The Myth of Youth Apathy: Young Europeans' Critical Attitudes toward Democratic Life." *American Behavioral Scientist* 58 (5): 645–64.

Collier, David, and Steven Levitsky. 1997. "Democracy with Adjectives: Conceptual Innovation in Comparative Research." *World Politics* 49: 430–51.

Downs, Anthony. 1957. *An Economic Theory of Democracy*. New York: Harper & Row.

Ekman, Joakim, and Erik Amnå. 2012. "Political Participation and Civic Engagement: Towards a New Typology." *Human Affairs* 22 (3): 283–300.

Gallie, Walter B. 1956. "Essentially Contested Concepts." *Proceedings of the Aristotelian Society* 56: 167–98.

Hay, Colin. 2007. *Why We Hate Politics*. Cambridge: Polity Press.

Hempel, Carl G. 1965. *Aspects of Scientific Explanation and Other Essays in the Philosophy of Science*. New York: Free Press.

Hooghe, Marc, and Ellen Quintelier. 2014. "Political Participation in European Countries: The Effect of Authoritarian Rule, Corruption, Lack of Good Governance and Economic Downturn." *Comparative European Politics* 12 (2): 209–32.

Inglehart, Ronald. 1977. *The Silent Revolution: Changing Values and Political Styles among Western Publics*. Princeton: Princeton University Press.

———. 1990. *Culture Shift in Advanced Industrial Society*. Princeton: Princeton University Press.

Karpf, David. 2010. "Online Political Mobilization from the Advocacy Group's Perspective: Looking beyond Clicktivism." *Policy & Internet* 2 (4): 7–41.

Lilleker, Darren G, and Karolina Koc-Michalska. 2017. "What Drives Political Participation? Motivations and Mobilization in a Digital Age." *Political Communication* 34 (1): 21–43.

Macedo, Stephen, Yvette Alex-Assensoh, Jeffrey M Berry, Michael Brintnall, David E Campbell, Luis Ricardo Fraga, Archon Fung, et al. 2005. *Democracy at Risk: How Political Choices Undermine Citizen Participation and What We Can Do about It*. Washington, DC: Brookings Institution Press.

McCaughey, Martha, and Michael D Ayers. 2003. *Cyberactivism: Online Activism in Theory and Practice*. New York: Routledge.

Micheletti, Michele. 2003. *Political Virtue and Shopping: Individuals, Consumerism and Collective Action*. New York: Palgrave Macmillan.

Micheletti, Michele, and Dietlind Stolle. 2010. "Vegetarianism—A Lifestyle Politics?" In *Creative Participation: Responsibility-Taking in the Political World*, edited by Michele Micheletti and Andrew S McFarland, 125–45. Boulder: Paradigm Publishers.

Milbrath, Lester W. 1965. *Political Participation: How and Why Do People Get Involved in Politics*. Chicago: Rand McNally.

New Statesman. 2015. "What Is the Point of Changing Your Facebook Profile Picture to a French Flag?" *New Statesman*. www.newstatesman.com/science-tech/social-media/2015/11/what-point-changing-your-facebook-profile-picture-french-flag.

The Nation. 2001. "My Nike Media Adventure." *The Nation*, March. www.thenation.com/article/my-nike-media-adventure/.

Norris, Pippa. 2002. *Democratic Phoenix: Reinventing Political Activism*. Cambridge: Cambridge University Press.

Parry, Geraint, George Moyser, and Neil Day. 1992. *Political Participation and Democracy in Britain*. Cambridge: Cambridge University Press.

Penney, Joel. 2015. "Social Media and Symbolic Action: Exploring Participation in the Facebook Red Equal Sign Profile Picture Campaign." *Journal of Computer-Mediated Communication* 20 (1): 52–66.

Rojas, Hernando, and Eulalia Puig-I-Abril. 2009. "Mobilizers Mobilized: Information, Expression, Mobilization and Participation in the Digital Age." *Journal of Computer-Mediated Communication* 14 (4): 902–27.

Ryan, Richard M, and Edward L Deci. 2000. "Intrinsic and Extrinsic Motivations: Classic Definitions and New Directions." *Contemporary Educational Psychology* 25 (1): 54–67.

Sartori, Giovanni. 1970. "Concept Misformation in Comparative Politics." *American Political Science Review* 64 (4): 1033–53.

Schlozman, Kay Lehman, Sidney Verba, and Henry E Brady. 2012. *The Unheavenly Chorus: Unequal Political Voice and the Broken Promise of American Democracy*. Princeton: Princeton University Press.

Stoker, Gerry. 2006. *Why Politics Matter: Making Democracy Work*. Houndmills and New York: Palgrave.

Stolle, Dietlind, Marc Hooghe, and Michele Micheletti. 2005. "Politics in the Supermarket: Political Consumerism as a Form of Political Participation." *International Political Science Review* 26 (3): 245–69.

Stolle, Dietlind, and Michele Micheletti. 2013. *Political Consumerism: Global Responsibility in Action.* Cambridge: Cambridge University Press.

Süddeutsche Zeitung. 2014. "Was, Wenn Er Anzug Getragen Hätte?" *Süddeutsche Zeitung*, August 13.

Teorell, Jan. 2010. *Determinants of Democratization: Explaining Regime Change in the World, 1972–2006.* Cambridge: Cambridge University Press.

Theocharis, Yannis. 2015. "The Conceptualization of Digitally Networked Participation." *Social Media + Society* 1 (2): 1–14.

Tilly, Charles, and Sidney Tarrow. 2006. *Contentious Politics.* Oxford: Oxford University Press.

Time. 2014. "#Dontshoot Protesters Outraged by Ferguson Teen's Death Throw Up Their Hands on Instagram." *Time.* time.com/3144731/ferguson-dontshoot.

van Deth, Jan W. 2014. "A Conceptual Map of Political Participation." *Acta Politica* 49 (3): 349–67.

———. 2016. "What Is Political Participation." In *Oxford Research Encyclopedia in Politics: Political Behavior.* Oxford: Oxford University Press. politics.oxfordre.com/view/10.1093/acrefore/9780190228637.001.0001/acrefore-9780190228637-e-68.

Verba, Sidney, and Norman H Nie. 1972. *Participation in America: Political Democracy and Social Equality.* Chicago: University of Chicago Press.

Verba, Sidney, Norman H Nie, and Jae-On Kim. 1978. *Participation and Political Equality: A Seven-Nation Comparison.* New York and London: University of Chicago Press.

Verba, Sidney, Kay Lehman Schlozman, and Henry E Brady. 1995. *Voice and Equality: Civic Voluntarism in American Politics.* Cambridge: Harvard University Press.

Zukin, Cliff, Scott Keeter, Molly Andolina, Krista Jenkins, and Michael X Delli Carpini. 2006. *A New Engagement? Political Participation, Civic Life, and the Changing American Citizen.* Oxford: Oxford University Press.

5 Measuring Old and New Forms of Political Participation

Observers note that some subjects in political science are exhaustively studied, generating many publications, while others are neglected. [. . .] The explanation is that data is already available on the popular subjects, whereas on the neglected ones one would have to leave one's computer and engage in onerous, low-tech information gathering out in the world.

(Mead 2010, 454)

5.1 A Fresh Look at Political Participation

Capturing new ways in which citizens engage in politics is one of the most important challenges facing empirical research on political participation. Obviously, this problem is strongly interlinked with the continuous growth of the repertoire of participation in democratic systems (see Chapter 2) and with the risk of arriving at a "concept of everything" outlined earlier (see Chapter 3). These two aspects are closely related: Actual expansions of the repertoire of participation can only be studied—or even perceived—successfully by using adequate conceptual specifications. Almost by definition, existing research tends to be inherently conservative; that is, it relies on standardized measures to facilitate cross-national as well as longitudinal comparisons. Although the advantages of this practice are evident, the major drawback is that new forms of participation are discarded. Consequently, discussions about the quality of democracies are based on the limited empirical evidence of citizens' engagement, and important parts of the picture may be missing from our explanations.

Acknowledging these challenges, the objective of this chapter is to offer a fresh empirical approach for measuring political participation. Building on the precise guidelines on how to identify a form of political participation in Chapter 4, we develop a new empirical approach that strikes a balance between having pre-defined instruments along with more open, citizen-led insights as to what qualifies as political participation. Using the conceptual map of participation, we identify new forms of political participation and integrate them in empirical analyses alongside other well-known and commonly used participatory forms. Such an approach is fertile for observing the staggering breadth of diverse acts that citizens understand, define, and employ as forms of participating in politics today. Besides, it is suitable for investigating how new forms of political participation are integrated within the broader structure of participation by developing a new taxonomy for the expanded repertoire of political participation. The core of the empirical arguments presented in this chapter is based on the results obtained from a special study we developed deploying this approach (Theocharis and van Deth 2016). The most important point being addressed is whether new forms of participation fit into a broader structure of political participation and, in this way, establish new *modes* of participation. Following the structural analysis, we explore the main antecedents of old and new modes of political participation detected.

5.2 Integrating Citizens' Input Into the Study of Participation

5.2.1 Using the Conceptual Map for a New Measurement Approach

The logic of our approach is based on the idea of collecting empirical evidence for activities that are conventionally understood as forms of political participation (i.e. voting, demonstrating, or signing petitions) along with evidence on newly arising forms of participation (i.e. blogging or guerrilla gardening). For each of these two categories a different research strategy seems to be required: Whereas acknowledged forms of participation can be measured by using a list of standardized items, new and emerging forms of participation are largely unknown. Because these last activities are frequently based on specific perceptions and motivations, the instrument should allow citizens to define their own activities as political participation. In order to meet these contradictory requirements, we designed a new instrument combining both strategies. First, a list of items sets the stage by mentioning activities that are conventionally understood as political participation. This list is then, second, followed by an open question that provides examples of participatory expansions and invites citizens to mention similar activities they might have been involved in. The order is key here. By offering first an extensive list of items and inviting respondents to go through that list and indicate for each form whether they have been engaged in it, empirical information about the typical repertoire of participation including a variety of more or less common political acts is efficiently obtained. By mentioning examples of expanded forms of participation immediately after the items on the list as an introduction to an open question, it is made clear that, by asking that additional question, the researcher is after activities that were not part of that previous list. This conveys a direct message to the respondent that he or she should not repeat any of the items of the list, but rather think in terms of expansions beyond these activities.

Which items should be on the list as specimen of forms of political participation? Answering this question was one of the main objectives of the conceptual map we developed in Chapter 4. This map resulted in five variants of forms of political participation in three main areas and so we need items representing each variant. To this end we included a diverse battery of participatory forms that cluster under different variants.

Political Participation-I: Minimal definition

The four decision rules for the minimal definition define the first variant of political participation as voluntary, non-professional activities that are located in the area of politics, government, or the state. Obviously, casting a vote is a major example of such activities. Other activities that are widely used in empirical research for this variant of political participation are these: contacting a politician, attending a political meeting, donating money to a political organization, and working for a party or a candidate. These five forms of participation establish the first set of items to be included in our instrument.

Political Participation-II: targeted at government, politics, or the state

Voluntary, non-professional activities that are not located in the political area, but are targeted towards government, politics, or the state, establish a second variant of forms of political participation. Major specimens of these activities selected for our instrument are these: signing a petition, demonstrating, and working for a political action group.

Political Participation-III: targeted at problems or community issues

The second variant of target definitions of forms of political participation covers voluntary, non-professional activities that are neither located in the political area nor are they directed towards government, politics, or the state. Instead, these activities deal with attempts to solve common problems or community issues. For our instrument, we selected three activities as relevant under this conception: donating money to a social, humanitarian or charitable organization; volunteering in such an organization; and volunteering for a community project.

Political Participation-IV: political context

Voluntary, non-professional activities that are neither located in the political area nor targeted at government, politics, or the state, and which are not attempts to solve (community) problems are usually difficult to recognize as forms of political participation. In these cases, contextual evidence might provide the clue to accept these activities as forms of political participation. Activities on digital media dealing with social or political issues present major examples of forms of participation that might be covered by this variant. For these forms, platform-enabled cues can provide clear information about the *political context* (e.g. #BlackLivesMatter) of seemingly non-political activities.[1] For our instrument we selected the following three activities that have been proposed and used by PEW (Smith 2013): posting or sharing links to political stories, commenting on social or political issues on social media, and encouraging other people to take action and a political or social issues using social media.

Political Participation-V: politically motivated

The last variant of forms of participation distinguished by the conceptual map are voluntary, non-professional activities that are neither located in the political area, nor targeted at government, politics, or the state, which do not attempt to solve (community) problems, and are not placed in a clear political context. If these non-political activities are politically motivated, then we are dealing with specimen of political participation. By now, the most common variant of these activities is the use of consumer power to express political opinions (Micheletti 2003). Instead of a single item on political consumerism we followed the recommendations of recent research in this area (Copeland 2014b; Zorell 2016) and included in our list boycotting certain products for political or ethical reasons and deliberately buying products for these reasons.

In order to avoid any suggestion about the nature, direction, or goal, the introductory sentence for the total set was restricted to the simple question: "During the last twelve months, have you done any of the following: . . ." with response categories "yes", "no", and "no answer/ refused to say". For voting, the last national election was referred to.

5.2.2 Measuring New Forms of Participation

The procedure outlined in the previous sub-section enables us to measure the use of broadly accepted forms of political participation among citizens by using a standardized format. Although this procedure does not exclude any phenomena a priori, we ended up with a list of 16 specific activities. How then can we account for arising new forms of participation and the use of non-political activities for political reasons? The map can, of course, be applied to categorize such phenomena, but it does not help us to identify them. If we want to know what activities citizens consider to be forms of political participation, our instrument should allow citizens to phrase their responses in their own words.

Scholars adopting different approaches have come up with alternative solutions for not imposing a definition of politics or participation to their respondents. In one such manifestation, O'Toole, Marsh, and Jones (2003, 351) asked their focus-groups members to freely associate with images, to discuss and, subsequently, to sort the images according to those they considered to be political and those which they did not. This approach is very valuable for focus groups but hard to apply to obtaining information from hundreds of citizens. Following the rationale of O'Toole, Marsh, and Jones (2003, 350), our objective is to enable respondents to freely relate to politics as an expanded or solely expressive activity they may have been engaged in. Placing an open question at the very end of the preconceived list of 16 participatory activities presumably increases the chances that the respondents would mention activities that they themselves loosely associate with political participation. The phenomena mentioned by our respondents could then be filtered through the conceptual map, allowing us to recognize whether these forms fit any of the definitions of political participation, and how they should be empirically treated. The following question was thus included in our instrument as a 17th item:

> In Berlin, a group of people planted flowers in abandoned sites without permission, in order to make their neighborhood more beautiful; In Vienna hundreds helped creating a miniature model of a city that could have been built instead of bailing out banks. In Ferguson, thousands shared photos on social media to protest the shooting of a young black man by a white policeman. Many other examples of such expressive actions can be thought of and these are only three examples. During the last twelve months, have you been engaged in any such actions to express your political or social views or concerns?

All respondents confirming this question were asked: "what did you do?" and the interviewer wrote down up to three responses.

The wording we selected for this additional question draws on different acts, carried in different contexts, and by different people. The question thus embeds a variation of hard-to-define-as-political acts that range from guerrilla gardening—one of many do-it-yourself (DIY) urban activities employed nowadays for the beautification of cities—to creative and collective acts such as urban architecture, and acts that take place solely online and are enabled by social media. By mentioning different incidents or events taking place in diverse cities, the question also clearly prompts the respondent to relate to activities that, on the one hand, extend beyond conventional understandings of participation but that, on the other hand, may be shared with others elsewhere as a collective expression about an issue.

5.3 A New Taxonomy of Political Participation

The new instrument to measure political participation has been designed on the basis of the ascertainment of the continuously expanding repertoire of political participation (Chapter 2) and the theoretical considerations underlying the conceptual map (Chapter 4). Next, we designed a short survey to test the usefulness of our instrument and to see how old and new forms of participation together determine the repertoire of participation. To put this strategy into action, a representative sample of the German population (age 18 and older) was invited to answer our 17 questions on participation, as well as some additional questions on their political orientations and socio-demographic features (see Appendix for the precise phrasing of questions on political participation). A survey agency carried out tele-phone interviews (CATI) between 17 April and 9 May 2015, with an average duration of 8.4 minutes.[2] A total of 1004 interviews are avail-able for analysis (response rate 20.2 percent).

5.3.1 Results of the Open Question, Identification of Participatory Acts, and Coding Procedure

The survey provided straightforward responses to the 16 standardized participation (yes/no) items. In addition, a total number of 101 respon-dents (10.1 percent) indicated that they had been engaged in actions aimed at expressing political or social views or concerns similar to the ones mentioned in the introductory text to the open question. A brief look at the ESS data from Germany collected only somewhat earlier (ESS Round 7 2014) shows that such activities are more popular than a number of institutionalized and extra-institutionalized acts, includ-ing working in a political party or action group (4.5 percent), wearing or displaying a campaign badge or sticker (9 percent), and taking part in a lawful public demonstration (7.5 percent)—but not as popular as contacting a politician or government (16 percent) or signing petitions (22 percent). Of the 101 respondents who used the open-ended ques-tion, 90 mentioned a single action or cause (remainders used "don't know", or refused to provide specific answers), whereas 16 respon-dents mentioned two, and four people even mentioned three actions or causes. As a result, the interviewers wrote down 110 actions or causes. Before we can analyze the structure of the repertoire of politi-cal participation, these responses to the open-ended questions have to be identified as participatory acts and subsequently coded.

The respondents' answers pointed towards a staggering variety of participatory activities and included anything from beautifying a mar-ketplace with flowers, planting on one's street and spreading seedbombs across vacant land, to remembrance ceremonies for refugee victims in the Mediterranean, a balloon action for lesbian and gay rights, and performing games in protest against too little separation of church and state in Germany. This small sample shows that none of the activi-ties mentioned fits commonly used definitions of political participa-tion such as "activities by private citizens that are more or less directly aimed at influencing the selection of governmental personnel and/or the actions they take" (Verba and Nie 1972, 2). To the contrary, most of these activities are separated from the locus of politics: they make cre-ative use of the urban space, they address through *direct action*—rather than through representatives—issues such as the refugee tragedy in the

Mediterranean, lesbian and gay rights, and urban decay; and some do not have a clear recipient or target who should presumably change or enact policies as a result on these acts (certainly not an institutional-ized one). Does this mean that these acts do not qualify as political participation? To tackle this conceptual question, we followed the same procedure as was illustrated in Table 4.1 (Chapter 4); that is, for each activity mentioned, we applied the decision rules provided in the con-ceptual map. Table 5.1 shows the results of this procedure for several activities mentioned by the respondents.

Once the different phenomena brought to our attention by our respondents have been identified as forms of political participation, the next step is to investigate how these forms fit within a repertoire of political participation. Do these new phenomena cluster empirically under one (or even more than one) new mode of participation, or are they merely new manifestations of "old" modes of participation whose existence previous literature already established (see Chapter 2)? In order to make the actions mentioned accessible for quantitative analyses, a coding and recoding procedure including two steps was developed. First, all actions mentioned that were already unmistak-ably covered by one of the 16 closed questions were deleted from the list of additional forms of participation, and were instead coded under the correct form. For instance, the answer "Petition to ban dangerous dogs" was recoded under the item "Signed a petition".[3] Secondly, all general references to "actions" or "protests" were coded as additional, new modes of participation, because the respondents already had the opportunity to recall such actions under one or more of the previous items related to protests. For instance, the answer "Action: roundtable for refugees" is apparently perceived as an additional form of partici-pation and therefore it has been coded as such. The same applies to answers whose specific form is less clear, such as "Local action against Nazis" or in case a further clarification is refused by the respondent. Only if the respondent confirms an additional activity in general, but does not know how to specify it, the response is not considered to be an expression of partaking in an additional form of participation. As a result of this procedure, we constructed a new variable that reflects these additional forms of political participation ("other") with 52 (5.0 percent) of the respondents having used it.

5.3.2 *The Variety of Participation*

Figure 5.1 shows the relative number of people involved in each of the 17 forms of participation used in this study (Theocharis and van

Table 5.1 Using the conceptual map to identify political activities mentioned

Participatory phenomenon	Rule								Classification
	1	2	3	4	5	6	7	8	
	activity?	voluntary?	non-professional?	locus: pol/gov/state?	target: pol/gov(state)?	target: probl/comm?	political context?	politically motivated?	
Planting one's own street	x	x	x	-	-	x	→		Political Participation-III (targeted definition: community)
Spreading seedbombs across vacant urban land	x	x	x	-	-	x	→		Political Participation-III (targeted definition: community)
Ceremony for refugee victims in the Mediterranean	x	x	x	-	-	-	x	→	Political Participation-IV (circumstantial definition: context)
Games in protest against too little separation of church and state	x	x	x	-	-	x	→		Political Participation-III (targeted definition: problem)
Balloon action in support for lesbian and gay rights	x	x	x	-	-	-	x	→	Political Participation-IV (circumstantial definition: motivation)
Panel discussion on the equality of homosexuality	x	x	x	-	-	x	→		Political Participation-III (targeted definition: problem)
Taking part in a rehabilitation project for child soldiers	x	x	x	-	-	x	→		Political Participation-III (targeted definition: problem)
Preserving a community garden project	x	x	x	-	-	x	→		Political Participation-III (targeted definition: community)
Participated in a demonstration against Nazis	x	x	x	-	x	→			Political Participation II (targeted definition: politics)

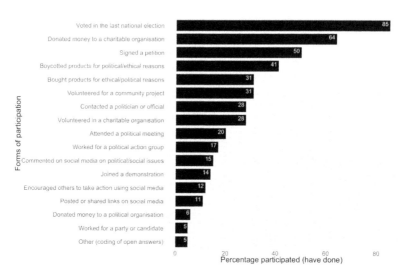

Figure 5.1 Frequencies of forms of participation (cases weighted by design weight)

Deth 2016).[4] The general pattern of these frequencies is in line with the results of similar studies in Germany and many other advanced democracies: Whereas voting still is, by far, the most used form of participation, other activities involving party work and political donations are at the very end of the distribution with only tiny parts of the population using these forms (Gabriel and Völkl 2005; Teorell, Torcal, and Montero 2007).

The percentage of people using forms of participation that we have designated as "other" is also limited (although no less popular than working for a party or candidate). Much more substantial parts of the population have been involved in activities such as signing a petition or boycotting products. Notably, the three forms of digitally networked participation—perhaps the most popular new forms of participation encountered in the literature—are also in the lower end of the graph, and have been done by modest percentages of the population only (11–15 percent).[5]

With the large number of different participation forms mentioned, it does not come as a surprise that only very few Germans (4 percent) have not been involved in any of the activities mentioned. Similarly, only few people (8 percent) indicate that they have used 10 or more of these forms. The average number of forms used is 4.64 (st. dev. = 2.97).

If casting a vote in the last national election is not taken into account this figure drops to 3.79 forms (st. dev. = 2.88; Theocharis and van Deth 2016, 11).

5.3.3 The Structure of Old and New Forms of Participation

Do new forms of participation establish a distinct new mode of political participation, or are they merely different manifestations of already existing modes? In order to answer this question empirically, internal and external validation strategies are applied here. First, the internal validation strategy focuses on the latent structure for the 17 items used to measure distinct forms of participation. A structure underlying these responses should present a conceptually convincingly taxonomy of the main modes of political participation. Second, the external strategy is based on the idea of "nomological networks" (Cronbach and Meehl 1955, 290), presuming that similar concepts should play the same role or perform the same function in broader explanations. For our modes of participation this implies that major antecedents should all show well-known relationships; that is, individual resources and attitudes, such as value orientations, satisfaction with democracy, and support of active citizenship, should be relatively strongly correlated with distinct modes of political participation.

Latent-Structure Analyses

To establish a taxonomy of political participation, we subjected all 17 forms of political participation to principal component analysis (PCA). Our dimensional analysis reveals a clear, latent structure with five components. Two items, however, do not fit into this structure. Neither "voting in the last national election" nor "donating money to a charitable organization" reaches satisfactory loadings in the rotated component matrix. Whereas many studies have shown the special character of voting as a distinct form of political participation (see, for instance, the discussion in Parry, Moyser, and Day 1992, 50–52), donating money apparently does not belong to the repertoire of political participation either. Given the dichotomous nature of the items, we performed a second PCA based on tetrachoric correlations. Unsurprisingly, a positive definite matrix could only be obtained by deleting "voting" from the analysis. Although four components can be derived with an eigenvalue greater than 1.0, inspecting the explained variances for the distinct components indicates that five components provide a more appropriate solution (the fifth component showing an eigenvalue of .998). The two PCAs—based on product-moment and tetrachoric correlations—provide exactly the same results, with "voting" and "donating money" as the two items that do not fit clearly in the configurations obtained. Table 5.2 shows the structure based on tetrachoric correlations (Theocharis and van Deth 2016, 13).[6]

The five components revealed by the analyses together shape a taxonomy of political participation with: (1) the four forms dealing with parties, politicians and political meetings indicating a mode we call "Institutionalized participation", (2) the three forms of digitally networked activities representing a mode called "Digitally networked participation" (DNP), (3) four forms of protest participation including the additional coded activities ("other") representing a mode called "Protest", (4) two items on "Volunteering", and (5) two items on "Consumerist participation".

These analyses lead to two important conclusions. First, digitally networked participation, perhaps the most popular and most debated of the emerging forms of participation, is very clearly not an expansion of an existing mode of participation, but a more fundamental enlargement of the repertoire with a distinct mode of participation. Second, the creative, expressive, and individualized forms of participation that our respondents provided appear to play a less innovative role: They broaden the already available protest dimension and are, in this way, integrated in one of the already existing modes.

The detection of a new mode of participation covering digitally networked participation is an important contribution to our understanding of online participation. As most of these activities rely on newly available technological opportunities only—and do not reflect online versions of previous forms—they can be perceived as new participatory phenomena. Yet, a suspicious reader may remain unconvinced that DNP is actually a mode of participation and argue that, since no other internet activities were included in our analysis, we may be simply capturing online activities in general, and not necessarily a new participatory dimension that has been *enabled* by social-media tools. Previous research, however, provides grounds to presume that not only certain online acts in general (Oser, Hooghe, and Marien 2013, 98), but digitally networked forms in particular, establish a distinct mode of political participation. In one of the few studies addressing this question, Gibson and Cantijoch (2013, 714) show that online forms of engagement that "take a more active, collective, and networked quality in the online environment" are indeed independent of offline and other online acts, concluding that "there is evidence that the medium matters". The results of our analyses corroborate this finding by showing

Table 5.2 Structure of political participation (PCA based on tetrachoric correlations; only coefficients >.40 reported)

	Institutionalized	DNP	Protest	Volunteering	Consumerist
Worked for a party or candidate	.864				
Donated money to a political organisation	.808				
Attended a political meeting	.795				
Contacted a politician or official	.670				
Commented on social media on political/social issues		.906			
Posted or shared political links on social media		.859			
Encouraged other people to take action using social media		.809			
Signed a petition			.809		
Worked for a political action group			.728		
Joined a demonstration			.527		
Other (coded open answers)			.524		
Volunteered in a charitable organisation				.872	
Volunteered for a community project				.838	
Bought products for political/ethical reasons					.895
Boycotted products for political/ethical reasons					.844
Donated money to a charitable organisation					

Varimax with Kaiser-Normalisation; matrix of tetrachoric correlations for 17 items not positive definite, therefore "voting" is deleted from the analyses. Explained variance: 67 per cent; N = 1004 that three quintessentially social-media enabled acts cluster together under the umbrella of digitally networked participation and establish a distinct mode of participation within the general repertoire.[7]

Measuring Old and New Modes of Participation

For each of the five distinct modes of political participation revealed by our dimensional analysis, levels of participation are computed based on additive scores corrected for the number of items included (resulting in standardized 0–1 scales). The percentages of those who have engaged in each one of those five activities, as well as in electoral participation, are shown in Figure 5.2 (Theocharis and van Deth 2016, 14). Electoral participation is by far the most popular mode of participation with 85 percent of our sample engaging in this act. Protest participation comes second (57 percent) followed by consumerist participation (48 percent) and volunteering (41 percent). Institutionalized participation (37 percent) is the second least popular mode of participation followed by DNP (22 percent). Perhaps the most important insight offered by these figures is that the highest levels of non-electoral participation are observed not only in protest activities—which fit well within existing definitions of participation—but also in the two modes of participation that lack a clear political connotation (consumerism and volunteering). This finding adds evidence to a growing literature

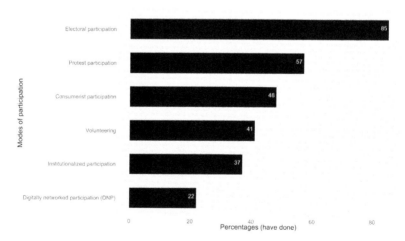

Figure 5.2 Levels of participation for distinct modes (cases weighted by design weight)

demonstrating the popularity of non-institutionalized, community-oriented, and lifestyle-driven participation, as opposed to engagement through traditional political avenues such as political parties (see, for instance, Stolle, Hooghe, and Micheletti 2005; Zukin et al. 2006; Dalton and Wattenberg 2000). Although DNP shows the lowest level of involvement with one out of five citizens using this mode of participation, this percentage certainly cannot be neglected.

The overall six (including voting) modes of participation are all moderately but positively correlated with each other, with bivariate product-moment correlations ranging from .09 for electoral participation and protest, to .33 for protest and institutionalized participation. Apparently, the modes of participation are not used separately—being involved in one mode of participation increases the chances of using other modes too. This finding echoes previous research showing that, for those who participate in politics, the new modes investigated here do not replace older modes of participation but rather complement citizens' repertoires (Van Laer and Van Aelst 2010; Norris 2002; Oser 2017). The single exception in this picture is provided by the relationship between casting a vote and engaging in DNP: Of the 15 bivariate correlations for the six modes of participation, only this coefficient is very modest and negative (-.014). Besides, only this estimate does not reach an acceptable level of statistical significance (p < .01; two-tailed). This result could be due to the fact that it concerns the relationship between the most and least frequently used modes of participation, thus reducing the chances to obtain a positive correlation. However, non-parametric correlation coefficients (Tau-b and Rho) for this relationship are very modest but positive, but are also non-significant (p < .01; two-tailed). All these estimations suggest that voting and DNP probably do not come together; that is, being involved in one of these two modes of participation does not influence the chances of using the other mode too.

Antecedents of Old and New Modes of Political Participation

Political science researchers have long established a number of well-known predictors of different modes of political participation (Verba, Schlozman, and Brady 1995; Schlozman, Verba, and Brady 2012; van Deth, Montero, and Westholm 2007). Yet, less is known about the extent to which newer modes share similar predictors. If we are dealing with similar concepts, then structural similarities between the "nomological networks" for various modes of political participation should be evident (Theocharis and van Deth 2016). To investigate this, given the distributional properties of the additive participation scales, we first recoded all dependent variables as binary variables (except from voting which is already binary). In this way, each variable indicates whether a respondent had made use of at least one of the forms of participation belonging to a certain mode. Subsequently we estimated logistic regression models for all six modes of political participation. Scores for each mode are regressed in two steps: first by using only individual resources (gender, education, age, and age squared[8]) and, next, by adding typical attitudinal variables predicting participation (value orientations, satisfaction with democracy, left-right self-placement), as well as support for a relevant norm of citizenship (being active in politics; Dalton 2008b).[9]

The regression results shown in Table 5.3 corroborate findings from previous research. Resources (see the first models for each mode of participation) are, give or take, significant antecedents of participation. The impact of higher education is consistently statistically significant in every model, whereas gender (men) significantly increases the probability of engaging in digitally networked, institutionalized, and protest acts. This is not the case for consumerist acts, however, as women have a higher probability to engage in these activities. This finding has been corroborated in a number of studies on new forms of political participation (Stolle and Micheletti 2013; Stolle and Hooghe 2011; Copeland 2014a). Age appears to be relevant for voting, consumerism, and volunteering. Although it is clear that being older means that one has a higher probability of turning out to vote, the two other modes also display a curvilinear relationship; that is, the probability of engaging in consumerist and protest participation acts increases with age, but is relatively low among both the younger and the older groups. Interestingly, and in line with recent studies conducted in the US (Feezell 2016), in our models restricted to resource-related determinants, age is unrelated to digitally networked participation and to volunteering. These findings provide support for the argument that young people—a group historically less likely to be involved in politics through institutionalized participatory avenues (Schlozman, Verba, and Brady 2012)—are not less engaged compared to older groups when it comes to these modes of participation. Community-based and networked forms of participation may thus present opportunities for political engagement for this age group (Zukin et al. 2006; Xenos, Vromen, and Loader 2014).

Looking at the AIC values, it is evident that, once attitudinal variables are added (and the number of cases is held constant at 929), every model as a whole fits significantly better than a model only including

Table 5.3 Antecedents of six modes of political participation (logistic regressions)

	DNP		Institutionalized		Consumerist		Protest		Volunteering		Voting	
	(1)	(2)	(3)	(4)	(5)	(6)	(7)	(8)	(9)	(10)	(11)	(12)
Gender	-0.284 (0.160)	-0.359* (0.169)	-0.643*** (0.135)	-0.750*** (0.148)	0.533*** (0.137)	0.493*** (0.147)	-0.170 (0.133)	-0.280* (0.142)	-0.147 (0.132)	-0.191 (0.139)	-0.168 (0.189)	-0.202 (0.209)
Education	1.320*** (0.312)	1.345*** (0.334)	1.281*** (0.259)	1.154*** (0.282)	2.034*** (0.262)	1.835*** (0.280)	1.215*** (0.252)	1.002*** (0.269)	1.340*** (0.253)	1.158*** (0.267)	1.835*** (0.363)	1.403*** (0.399)
Age	-2.728 (2.101)	-3.030 (2.233)	3.570* (1.717)	3.484 (1.857)	7.890*** (1.793)	7.250*** (1.902)	3.630* (1.669)	2.653 (1.776)	1.042 (1.657)	1.095 (1.738)	5.208* (2.289)	6.842** (2.485)
Age squared	-0.174 (2.502)	-0.111 (2.662)	-3.530 (1.897)	-3.638 (2.060)	-9.949*** (2.021)	-9.436*** (2.148)	-4.996** (1.847)	-4.046* (1.965)	-1.268 (1.836)	-1.516 (1.931)	-2.871 (2.683)	-4.542 (2.911)
Values: Mixed		-0.227 (0.396)		0.159 (0.376)		0.354 (0.348)		-0.012 (0.323)		0.342 (0.344)		-0.560 (0.481)
Values: Postmaterialist		0.306 (0.396)		0.676 (0.378)		0.928** (0.352)		0.533 (0.329)		0.409 (0.348)		-0.502 (0.492)
Satisfaction with democracy		-0.763 (0.392)		0.286 (0.344)		0.364 (0.348)		0.191 (0.335)		0.524 (0.330)		1.646*** (0.475)
Left/right placement		-0.326 (0.442)		-0.029 (0.371)		-1.243*** (0.371)		-0.316 (0.353)		-0.122 (0.350)		-0.481 (0.526)
Good citizen norm: Active in politics		1.094** (0.390)		2.293*** (0.348)		0.894** (0.328)		1.246*** (0.317)		1.028** (0.315)		2.185*** (0.449)

(Continued)

Table 5.3 (Continued)

	DNP		Institutionalized		Consumerist		Protest		Volunteering		Voting	
	(1)	(2)	(3)	(4)	(5)	(6)	(7)	(8)	(9)	(10)	(11)	(12)
Constant	-0.828** (0.311)	-0.756 (0.616)	-1.408*** (0.288)	-3.163*** (0.576)	-1.934*** (0.293)	-2.415*** (0.540)	-0.361 (0.273)	-0.949 (0.508)	-1.152*** (0.277)	-2.199*** (0.526)	-0.430 (0.338)	-1.722* (0.712)
Observations	985	929	985	929	985	929	985	929	985	929	985	929
Log Likelihood	-486.735	-450.796	-632.063	-563.740	-624.310	-563.941	-643.015	-588.318	-653.026	-609.616	-376.759	-318.703
Akaike Inf. Crit.	983.470	921.592	1,274.126	1,147.480	1,258.621	1,147.881	1,296.029	1,196.636	1,316.051	1,239.232	763.518	657.405

Note: $*p < 0.05$; $**p < 0.01$; $***p < 0.001$

resources. Supporting postmaterialist values, theoretically a predictor of all—and not just new—forms of participation, only increases the probability of consumerist activities, whereas those identifying with the left also have a higher propensity to participate in such activities. Furthermore, people more satisfied with democracy have a higher propensity to vote.

Support for the norm "being active in politics" is an important element of good citizenship. This indicator is the only attitudinal variable that shows consistently statistically significant coefficients across all models: Citizens who support this norm are likely to participate in old as well as in new forms of engagement. This finding is particularly interesting because it illustrates that new modes of participation share with well-established forms of political participation a "core" predictor linked to the normative idea that being politically active is an aspect of good citizenship. Figure 5.3 displays the predicted probabilities[10] of participating in the different modes of participation examined in this study (Theocharis and van Deth 2016, 19). Looking at the probabilities of participating in digitally networked, consumerist, and voluntary acts, it becomes clear that those who believe that a good citizen should be active in politics have a higher propensity to engage in all three of the modes that lack an unambiguous political connotation—just as it is the case with the three classic modes of political participation (voting, institutionalized participation, and protest).[11] In short, the findings support the idea that digitally networked participation shares, to a very large extent, similar predictors with older modes of participation whose political nature is not challenged.

Our empirical findings speak also to the debate about the potential of digitally networked participation to ameliorate participatory inequalities. The full models display a relatively similar pattern to the findings presented by Schlozman, Verba, and Brady (2012, 532). Well-established socio-economic inequalities with regards to gender and education are both replicated for digitally networked participation. That is, better-educated men have a relatively higher probability to engage in digitally networked participation than lower-educated women, just as it is the case with every other activity except consumerist participation.[12] Importantly, however, age-based participatory inequalities do seem to be ameliorated in Germany as age is irrelevant for this type of participation. As others have alluded (Xenos, Vromen, and Loader 2014), this could mean that, if popularization of these forms of participation continues to grow, then digitally networked participatory opportunities may help bring new people to the political arena that were previously politically disengaged.

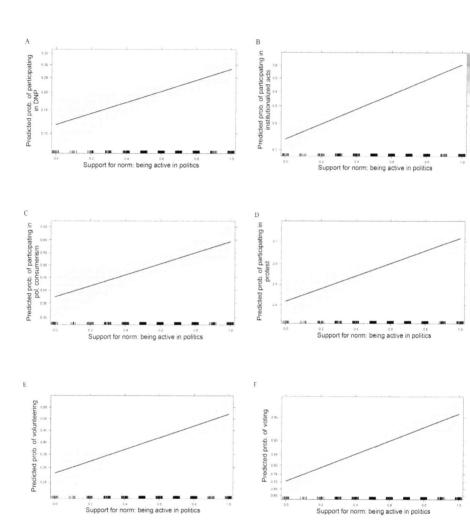

Figure 5.3 Support for norm "being active in politics" and predicted probabilities of participating in six modes of participation

5.4 From Activities to a New Taxonomy

Following the map of political participation proposed in Chapter 4, our objective in this chapter was threefold. First, to demonstrate how the conceptual map of participation can be used for ensuring that one's instrument consists of various well-known and widely used forms of political participation. Acknowledging that existing instruments for measuring political participation are not adequate for measuring creative and expressive political behaviors that may occur irregularly, under specific *contexts* and based on specific *motivations*, we propose, second, a new approach to measuring political participation. After asking people to indicate whether they have used common forms of participation, we used an open-ended question. The conceptual map allowed us to identify these acts reported as specific forms of participation. The third objective was to empirically examine how the new forms of participation revealed by our proposed measurement procedure fit within a broader structure of participation, and how their main antecedents compare to other, well-known forms of political participation.

The various steps in this strategy as well as the main findings are summarized in Table 5.4. Starting with the five major types of political participation as defined by the conceptual map of participation, we selected a number of typical specimens for each of these types (listed in the left-hand part of Table 5.4). By definition, emerging modes of participation cannot be covered by the 16 selected items. The right-hand side of the table presents the empirical findings and re-groups the initially selected items as well as the answers to the open-ended question. As can be seen the empirical results require a split for **Political Participation-I**, with voting being separated from other institutionalized forms of participation. Besides, donating money is not part of this mode of participation. More importantly, we see that the creative and expressive activities revealed by our open-ended question are part of the protest dimension (and of **Political Participation-II**) and that digitally networked activities establish their own mode of participation (covering **Political Participation-IV**). The conceptual and empirical parts of the table (left-hand and right-hand parts) are not linked directly: They both have their own logic and selection principles; that is, conceptual and empirical results can be related to each other but always require additional arguments.

The results of this combined, conceptually driven empirical investigation are revealing. Aside from engaging in well-known participatory acts, we find that citizens engage in a wide variety of acts that do not

Table 5.4 Summary of the conceptual (left-hand side) and empirical (right-hand side) strategies used

	Conceptual/theoretical part		Empirical part		
Using the conceptual made results in major variants of participation:	Major specimen of each of these variants and items used for empirical analyses:	Detected modes of participation in a new taxonomy:	Forms of participation included:		Use of each mode in Germany:
Political Participation-I	• casting a vote • contacting a politician • attending a political meeting • donating money to a political organisation • working for a party or a candidate	*Voting*	• casting a vote		85%
		Institutionalized participation	• contacting a politician • attending a political meeting • working for a party or a candidate		37%
Political Participation-II	• signing a petition • demonstrating • working for a political action group	*Protest*	• signing a petition • demonstrating • working for a political action group • other creative or expressive form (open-ended question)		57%

(*Continued*)

Table 5.4 (Continued)

Political Participation-III	• donating money to a social, humanitarian or charitable organisation • volunteering in a social, humanitarian or charitable organisation • volunteering for a community project	*Volunteering*	• donating money to a social, humanitarian or charitable organisation • volunteering in a social, humanitarian or charitable organisation • volunteering for a community project	41%
Political Participation-IV	• posting or sharing links to political stories on social media • commenting on social or political issues on social media • encouraging other people to take action and a political or social issues using social media	*Digitally networked participation (DNP)*	• posting or sharing links to political stories on social media • commenting on social or political issues on social media • encouraging other people to take action and a political or social issues using social media	22%
Political Participation-V	• boycotting certain products for political or ethical reasons • deliberatively buying products for political or ethical reasons	*Consumerist participation*	• boycotting certain products for political or ethical reasons • deliberatively buying products for political or ethical reasons	48%

fit available definitions of political participation widely used in the literature. Yet, many such acts can be classified as forms of political participation when taking into consideration the context within which they take place, or the motivation of the participants. These expansions of the repertoire of participation demonstrate the utility of the conceptual map we proposed for identifying all kinds of activities as forms of political participation, as opposed to the use of narrow definitions and missing out on a range of important phenomena. These phenomena appear to be well-integrated into a taxonomy of political participation consisting of six modes: volunteering, voting, institutionalized participation, political consumerism, protest, and digitally networked participation. That being said, two important and innovative insights arise that are important for the future study of political participation.

The first insight is that most of the phenomena captured by our open-ended question as novel ways of engaging in politics do not create a new mode of participation, but rather cluster under the existing protest mode. Given the diverse and creative nature of the phenomena we captured, this is a rather surprising finding. It would be interesting to study whether these forms establish a low-threshold, initial step—a "gateway" of sorts—into more conventional protest forms, such as demonstrating (for recent related research see Ekström and Shehata 2016). On the other hand, even a cursory look at these phenomena reveals that they are focused on direct action. In this sense, they fit within the broader context of political mobilization and political action associated with protesting. What merits further research, then, is the changing and expanding nature of protesting. When this phenomenon was brought into the focus of mainstream political science research in the late 1970s, the discussion surrounding its different manifestations focused on their legality, their legitimacy (Barnes et al. 1979, 45), its high costs, and its consequences for organizations (McAdam 1982; McCarthy and Zald 1977), whereas today the most debated features seem to be its individualistic, expressive, and seemingly non-political nature.

The second new insight is that digitally enabled forms of participation cluster together under a new mode of participation with no offline equivalents. Contrary to doubts and criticism about the extent to which digital forms of participation (or, for that matter, political consumerist activities) constitute a mode of political participation, many such acts qualify as political participation based on our conceptual system. Besides, citizens see them as much a part of their notion of politically engaged citizenship as they see any other conventional mode of participation.

Notes

1. Many of these forms can be classified under targeted as well as under circumstantial definitions if the text communicated provides sufficient information about the activity or its target. As has been indicated before (Chapter 4), the simplest definition (that is, a targeted definition) should be preferred.
2. The contacting strategy was based on the Gabler-Häder-Design, which is not limited to landlines but also includes mobile phones. This design is widely used for telephone interviewing in Germany and is certified by GESIS.
3. This shows that despite our efforts to strategically place the open-ended question after the list of acts we wanted our respondents to dissociate themselves from, the question was not able to fully achieve that objective. Still, a large variety of acts that have nothing to do with our closed questions were provided by the respondents.
4. All descriptive results presented here are based on computations weighted with dual-frame design weights taking into account the fact that we have a combination of fixed and mobile samples, resulting in composite selection probabilities.
5. This makes Germany a markedly different case compared to countries with highly developed and vibrant social-media cultures, such as the US or the UK. Already in 2013 the PEW Center (Smith 2013) reported percentages for these same acts in the US varying from 17 percent to 20 percent. As social media use for politics and news has increased significantly in the US (Gottfried and Shearer 2016), these US figures probably looked already very different at the time we conducted our study in Germany in 2015.
6. Results of confirmatory factor analyses are very similar to the results of the principal component analyses presented here. Apparently, the existence of five distinct dimensions underlying the 17 items does not depend on the technique chosen or the distributional properties of the data. Since the results of the component analyses can be presented straightforwardly we restrict the presentation to this latent structure here.
7. Using data from the Czech Republic and Greece (but with a different overall number of items due to survey limitations, and without an open-ended question) we have shown that the findings regarding the distinctness of DNP as a mode of participation within the broader repertoire are corroborated elsewhere too (Theocharis et al. 2016).
8. Although all findings hold with the inclusion of the income variable, given the high proportion of items missing from this variable (25 percent) we chose not to include income in the final models.
9. The item "being active in politics" gives us the opportunity to examine the correlation between a norm that refers directly to the importance of being active in politics and different activities, including those considered as lying beyond conventional understandings of political participation. This is an indirect way to demonstrate that new modes of participation may be perceived by citizens to be just as politically important for democratic engagement as well-established forms, and provide additional support to the idea that what citizens perceive as being part of politically active citizenship has changed (Bennett 2012; Dalton 2008a). For an extensive

discussion of these determinants and their operationalizations, see supplementary material in Theocharis and van Deth (2016).
10. Predicted probabilities were calculated keeping all other variables constant at their mean (continuous variables; 0 was used for dummy variables).
11. Given the distributional properties of our dependent variables, we also performed sensitivity checks using count models (Poisson regressions). The results follow a very similar pattern (see supplementary material in Theocharis and van Deth 2016).
12. Additional regression models including income, as well as sensitivity checks with count models, can be found in Theocharis and van Deth (2016, supplementary material).

References

Barnes, Samuel H, Max Kaase, Klaus R Allerbeck, Barbara G Farah, Felix Heunks, Ronald Inglehart, M Kent Jennings, Hans-Dieter Klingemann, Alan Marsh, and Leopold Rosenmayr. 1979. *Political Action: Mass Participation in Five Western Democracies*. Beverly Hills: Sage.

Bennett, Lance W. 2012. "The Personalization of Politics: Political Identity, Social Media, and Changing Patterns of Participation." *The ANNALS of the American Academy of Political and Social Science* 644 (1): 20–39.

Copeland, Lauren. 2014a. "Value Change and Political Action: Postmaterialism, Political Consumerism, and Political Participation." *American Political Research* 42 (2): 257–82.

———. 2014b. "Conceptualizing Political Consumerism: How Citizenship Norms Differentiate Boycotting from Buycotting." *Political Studies* 62 (1): 172–86.

Cronbach, Lee J, and Paul E Meehl. 1955. "Construct Validity in Psychological Tests." *Psychological Bulletin* 52 (4): 281–302.

Dalton, Russell. 2008a. *The Good Citizen: How a Younger Generation Is Reshaping American Politics*. Washington, DC: CQ Press.

———. 2008b. "Citizenship Norms and the Expansion of Political Participation." *Political Studies* 56 (1): 76–98.

Dalton, Russell, and Mark Wattenberg. 2000. *Parties without Partisans: Political Change in Advanced Industrial Democracies*. Oxford: Oxford University Press.

Ekström, Mats, and Adam Shehata. 2016. "Social Media, Porous Boundaries, and the Development of Online Political Engagement among Young Citizens." *New Media & Society*, 1–20. journals.sagepub.com/doi/10.1177/146144481 6670325.

ESS Round 7. 2014. "European Social Survey Round 7 Data." *European Social Survey Round 7 Data*. www.europeansocialsurvey.org/.

Feezell, Jessica T. 2016. "Predicting Online Political Participation: The Importance of Selection Bias and Selective Exposure in the Online Setting." *Political Research Quarterly* 69 (3): 495–509.

Gabriel, Oscar W, and Kerstin Völkl. 2005. "Politische und Soziale Partizipation." In *Die EU-Staaten im Vergleich*, edited by Oscar W Gabriel and Sabine Kropp, 268–98. Wiesbaden: VS Verlag für Sozialwissenschaften.

Gibson, Rachel, and Marta Cantijoch. 2013. "Conceptualizing and Measuring Participation in the Age of the Internet: Is Online Political Engagement Really Different to Offline?" *The Journal of Politics* 75 (3): 701–16.

Gottfried, Jeffrey, and Elisa Shearer. 2016. "News Use across Social Media Platforms 2016." Washington, DC. www.journalism.org/2016/05/26/news-use-across-social-media-platforms-2016/.

McAdam, Doug. 1982. *Political Process and the Development of Black Insurgency, 1930–1970*. 2nd Edition. Chicago, IL: University of Chicago Press.

McCarthy, John D, and Mayer N Zald. 1977. "Resource Mobilization and Social Movements: A Partial Theory." *American Journal of Sociology* 82 (6): 1212–41.

Mead, Lawrence M. 2010. "Scholasticism in Political Science." *Perspectives on Politics* 8 (2): 453–64.

Micheletti, Michele. 2003. *Political Virtue and Shopping: Individuals, Consumerism and Collective Action*. New York: Palgrave Macmillan.

Norris, Pippa. 2002. *Democratic Phoenix: Reinventing Political Activism*. Cambridge: Cambridge University Press.

Oser, Jennifer. 2017. "Assessing How Participators Combine Acts in Their 'Political Tool Kits': A Person-Centered Measurement Approach for Analyzing Citizen Participation." *Social Indicators Research* 133 (1): 235–258.

Oser, Jennifer, Marc Hooghe, and Sofie Marien. 2013. "Is Online Participation Distinct from Offline Participation? A Latent Class Analysis of Participation Types and Their Stratification." *Political Research Quarterly* 66 (1): 91–101.

O'Toole, Therese, David Marsh, and Su Jones. 2003. "Political Literacy Cuts Both Ways: The Politics of Non-Participation among Young People." *The Political Quarterly* 74 (3): 349–60.

Parry, Geraint, George Moyser, and Neil Day. 1992. *Political Participation and Democracy in Britain*. Cambridge: Cambridge University Press.

Schlozman, Kay Lehman, Sidney Verba, and Henry E Brady. 2012. *The Unheavenly Chorus: Unequal Political Voice and the Broken Promise of American Democracy*. Princeton: Princeton University Press.

Smith, Aaron. 2013. "Civic Engagement in the Digital Age." http://pewinternet.org/Reports/2013/Civic-Engagement.aspx.

Stolle, Dietlind, and Marc Hooghe. 2011. "Shifting Inequalities: Patterns of Exclusion and Inclusion in Emerging Forms of Political Participation." *European Societies* 13 (1): 119–42.

Stolle, Dietlind, Marc Hooghe, and Michele Micheletti. 2005. "Politics in the Supermarket: Political Consumerism as a Form of Political Participation." *International Political Science Review* 26 (3): 245–69.

Stolle, Dietlind, and Michele Micheletti. 2013. *Political Consumerism: Global Responsibility in Action*. Cambridge: Cambridge University Press.

Teorell, Jan, Mariano Torcal, and José Ramón Montero. 2007. "Political Participation: Mapping the Terrain." In *Citizenship and Involvement in European Democracies: A Comparative Analysis*, edited by Jan W van Deth, José Ramón Montero, and Anders Westholm, 334–57. London: Routledge.

Theocharis, Yannis, and Jan W van Deth. 2016. "The Continuous Expansion of Citizen Participation: A New Taxonomy." *European Political Science Review*. https://goo.gl/lYJtk7.

Theocharis, Yannis, Jan W van Deth, Peter Obert, and Ondřej Císař. 2016. "'We Came Unequal into This Digital World, and Unequal Shall We Go Out of It'? Digital Media and Participatory Inequality in Europe." *ECPR General Conference*. Prague, Czech Republic.

van Deth, Jan W, José Ramón Montero, and Anders Westholm (eds). 2007. *Citizenship and Involvement in European Democracies: A Comparative Analysis*. London: Routledge.

Van Laer, Jeroen, and Peter Van Aelst. 2010. "Internet and Social Movement Action Repertoires." *Information, Communication & Society* 13 (8): 1146–71.

Verba, Sidney, and Norman H Nie. 1972. *Participation in America: Political Democracy and Social Equality*. Chicago: University of Chicago Press.

Verba, Sidney, Kay Lehman Schlozman, and Henry E Brady. 1995. *Voice and Equality: Civic Voluntarism in American Politics*. Cambridge: Harvard University Press.

Xenos, Michael A, Ariadne Vromen, and Brian D Loader. 2014. "The Great Equalizer? Patterns of Social Media Use and Youth Political Engagement in Three Advanced Democracies." *Information, Communication & Society* 17 (2): 151–67.

Zorell, Carolin. 2016. "Varieties of Political Consumerism." PhD Dissertation. Universität Mannheim, Germany. ub-madoc.bib.uni-mannheim.de/42488.

Zukin, Cliff, Scott Keeter, Molly Andolina, Krista Jenkins, and Michael X Delli Carpini. 2006. *A New Engagement? Political Participation, Civic Life, and the Changing American Citizen*. Oxford: Oxford University Press.

6   A Road Map for the Study of Political Participation

> It is hardly surprising that the question of what are and are not legitimate acts of political participation has been and will continue to be a matter of conflict in day-to-day politics.
>
> (Barnes et al. 1979, 29)

6.1 Dealing With Political Participation Systematically

In the last decades, political participation has expanded, fragmented, and diversified so much that it is close to impossible to account for every participatory phenomenon. This development presents scholars—and, increasingly, politicians and organizers who are troubled with declining levels of conventional and civic participation—with a number of very important conceptual and practical questions. In this book, we have offered a conceptual and empirical fairway on how to study political engagement without excluding new forms of political participation by using dated conceptualizations while, at the same time, avoiding stretching concepts and instruments to cover almost everything. In the introductory chapter, we formulated four crucial questions to be answered:

1. Given the difficulty of detecting political acts that may not fit squarely within available definitions of participation, how do we recognize political participation if we see it?
2. In light of the expansion and the use of non-political activities for political purposes, how do we avoid falling into the trap of considering everything as participation?
3. (a) How can new forms of political participation be measured? And do they fit into a general taxonomy of participatory activities?
   (b) How widespread are new forms of political participation and who uses them?

4. How can our approach and findings be used by researchers who want to study new and emerging forms of political participation but do not want to exclude more conventional forms?

In this chapter, we use the insights offered by our study to briefly answer these four questions. In this way, a road map on how to study participation becomes available, with practical suggestions and recommendations for everybody confronted with the challenges of dealing with the rapidly expanding repertoires of political participation in a changing world.

6.2 How to Recognize Political Participation?

One of the most challenging tasks in the study of new forms of political participation today is to recognize the diverse participatory phenomena in the first place (Questions 1 and 2), and conceptualize them as participation. A major factor impeding these challenges, as we argued in Chapter 3, is the plurality of definitions of the concept of participation, ranging from very narrow ones to overly broad ones.

Rather than relying on too strict or too broad nominal definitions of participation, which are bound to either exclude many new and interesting phenomena, or consider as participation pretty much any activity under the sun, we have demonstrated that many of the conceptual problems can be solved through the use of a conceptual map. The major function of the map is not only to classify participatory acts systematically based on distinct features, but to help researchers identify a new phenomenon as a form of political participation based on its properties. This resolves the problem of "gray areas" and "increasing blurring of boundaries" presented by the growing popularity of modes of participation that do not meet conventional definitional criteria of political participation. Importantly, the rules that make up the map's structure lead to the identification of distinct features, which enable researchers to integrate contextual and motivational factors into the study of participatory phenomena, rather than be forced to ignore them or give them new labels, just because conventional definitions cannot accommodate these activities.

We have shown how an array of different phenomena, from strictly government-oriented activities to seemingly unpolitical activities, fit different definitional types of political participation (**Political Participation-I** to **-V**). The map, therefore, is not only useful for studying participation from the top-down (i.e. deciding which of the established measurement items to include in one's study) but, critically, from the bottom-up, by literally adjudicating on phenomena articulated by the participants themselves, and which would have otherwise remained unknown to the researcher. Applying the map, then, allows scholars to precisely define a phenomenon as a specific form of political participation—or as a non-political activity. In this way, the fallacy of considering everything as participation is avoided from the beginning without limiting the potential array of activities that can be studied as political participation.

6.3 Measuring Old and New Participatory Phenomena

Although a broad understanding of political participation is generally acknowledged, there has been no systematic effort to measure new forms of participation by examining their place in the broader repertoire of participation (Questions 3a and 3b). In Chapter 5, we have proposed a solution for addressing this challenge by combining open- and closed-ended questions. First, a list of items set the stage by mentioning activities that are conventionally understood as political participation. This is, second, followed by an open-ended question that provides examples of participatory expansions and invites citizens to mention similar activities they might have been involved in. By starting with an extensive list of items and inviting respondents to go through that list and indicate for each whether they have been engaged in it, empirical information about the typical repertoire of participation, including a variety of more or less common political acts, is efficiently obtained. The approach yielded several interesting insights which have been included in a new taxonomy of political participation covering six modes: (1) voting, (2) institutionalized participation, (3) digitally networked participation (DNP), (4) protest, (5) volunteering, and (6) consumerist participation.

This new taxonomy largely confirms available findings on the structure of political participation in advanced democracies. Yet, two findings presented in this book deserve special attention. The first one is that many participatory phenomena captured in our study do not represent a new mode of engaging in politics. To the contrary, all of these creative or expressive acts are part of the existing participatory mode of protesting. This result certainly requires further research on the particularities of protest: Why would these acts fit with protest and not, say, with boycotting, a mode of participation that is much more similar in terms of its distinctive identifying features?

The second major conclusion of our attempt to measure new forms of participation and integrate them into the broader participatory repertoire, is that digitally networked acts cluster together under a new mode of participation. Where exactly these acts stand empirically in comparison to other political acts has so far been less clear. Our study shows that digitally networked participation is indeed a new and distinct participatory phenomenon whose manifestations are already more popular than several manifestations of institutionalized and protest modes of participation. Perhaps most importantly, digitally networked acts share similar predictors with long-established modes of participation. A core takeaway message of these findings is that digitally networked participation cannot any longer remain in the side-lines of empirical social research. In order to avoid that social scientists miss important parts of democratic engagement, especially this type of participation should be included in large-scale surveys.

6.4 Future Expansions and Improvements

The dual strategy presented in this book provides practical solutions to conceptual and empirical problems of participation research (Question 4). Starting with conceptual challenges, the map can be used for many approaches to the study of political participation. For example, researchers interested in studying participatory phenomena can use the conceptual map in the preparatory phase of their research in order to establish clear features that the phenomena of interest should exhibit. This will be useful in quantitative approaches using, for example, surveys, before different acts are included in a questionnaire, or in qualitative approaches using, say, content analysis, in order to construct a codebook. There is increasing interest in social-media research in identifying how people talk about (or practice) political participation, and methodological proposals on how to use text to systematically detect participatory phenomena appearing in the (mainstream) media by using automated text analysis approaches (Brandt et al. 2017). The conceptual map can be an important part of initial stages of research designs aiming to explore participatory phenomena and their prevalence before heading into actual data collection.

The conceptual map can also be utilized inductively. Scholars who want to analyze survey data can employ the conceptual map for assessing participatory activities and establish criteria for inclusion in statistical analyses. Although the map's purpose is to identify forms of participation in a systematic way so that they can be used for assessing their prevalence, it does not necessarily *empirically* reflect five distinct dimensions of participation. As can be seen in Table 5.3, the conceptual and empirical structures overlap considerably. Yet this coherence is neither necessary nor is it in itself a positive sign. Conceptual and empirical approaches each have their own logics and rules. There are no direct connections between the two domains, and linking them requires extensive argumentations by (1) specifying theoretical concepts in empirical terms (operationalization) or by (2) interpreting empirical findings in theoretical terms (specification).

In qualitative research, the map can be used for classifying phenomena representing new forms of political participation coded through content analysis. The map could be of similar use in the coding of interviews or of focus group material, or in projects asking participants to discuss their political engagement through alternative avenues. Most importantly, perhaps, future research should take a step we have fallen short of taking in this book: examine more deeply the context in which these forms of engagement are embedded in. Although the conceptual map might look to some like a "dry" method for extracting definitions and classifying participation, it represents an opportunity for indicating broader areas, organizations, and events. An important related question is whether campaigns, be they political or social, play a strong role in making these new forms of participation available, or whether they are responding to them. If anything, the map shows that both old and new forms of participation do not happen in a vacuum, but are embedded within certain contexts or loci. These might be governmental, organizational, technological, or community-based contexts, and might be governed by distinct logics. Future work on new forms of political participation, therefore, should examine in detail contextual factors that are fertile for the emergence of such phenomena, and the characteristics of those involved in them.

Our combination of closed and open-ended questions to measure political participation provided a remarkably diverse list of ways through which citizens engage in politics. Even if relatively marginal in our country of study, these newly arising forms provide substantial information about the type of arenas in which citizens see politics materialize today and, at the same time, inform us about the shape-shifting of protest behavior in particular. They also highlight salient issues that people might be concerned about. In this sense, insight from approaches such as the one proposed in our study can yield information that are of particular interest to policy makers as well as to organizers, both in terms of helping them better understand citizens' concerns and to develop engagement techniques in their campaigns. With these advantages, our approach can be used to better understand new types of engagement into politics, their spread among the public and, in the end, their value for democracy. Clearly, the combination of the closed and open-ended questions is relatively difficult to implement in large-scale comparative surveys. That being said, save qualitative approaches such as in-depth interviews, which can extract such information, the procedure is short and straightforward for obtaining evidence about participatory phenomena from citizens themselves, rather than providing them with pre-defined behaviors. Importantly, the procedure is ideal for obtaining information from citizens in order to prepare material (such as measurement instruments) for inclusion in such large-scale surveys, especially if such studies show that certain phenomena are prevalent and important to citizens.

Finally, one of the most important aspects of our procedure is that, as long as the structure of the questions (i.e. first the closed and then the open-ended question) is kept consistent, the wording of the open-ended question can be altered, improved, and/or expanded to gain specific insights. Mentioning diverse participatory acts in the introduction can be modified through the use of examples that prompt the respondent to relate to phenomena specific to the researcher's interests, such as, say, environmental or lifestyle politics.

6.5 Finally: Why (and How) the Study of Old and New Forms of Participation Matters

Political science research has not kept pace with the increasing expansion of participation. Scores of new forms of political participation emerge on a daily basis. Some of them are online, others are offline; some are individualistic, others are collective; some are personalized by individuals, others are personalized by organizations; some are low cost, others entail extremely high costs; and some are visible, influential, and "go viral", whereas others are quiet and become known to little other than a small community of people. Many such phenomena have been overshadowed by the idea that they don't belong to the realm of politics, that "they don't make a difference", that they require too little effort, or simply because, although it would have been nice to know more about them, they were not included in the questionnaire. Although several scholars have singled out some such phenomena, no study has attempted to systematically conceptualize and classify them. As a result, the rise of new forms of political participation has been acknowledged by scholars, but it has scarcely gained greater prominence than a passing reference or a footnote cautioning that they should be investigated or included in future studies. Despite the ways in which different people and scholars understand and classify newly arising political phenomena, they represent acts in which citizens find important and potentially new ways to express their voice democratically. As some researchers have shown (Marsh, O'Toole, and Jones 2007), especially younger people value the democratic relevance of these activities.

Our approach to deal with the expansion of the repertoire of participation is pragmatic, not idealistic. We recognize that new forms of participation are emerging forms of engagement that have not taken off everywhere, nor are they as popular as many conventional acts. As it would be disproportional to treat them as the new formidable force in citizen engagement, it would be equally unproductive—and, indeed, misguided—to treat them solely as marginal phenomena. That the rise of new forms of participation coincides with the well-documented decline of institutionalized forms of participation, implies that citizens—who trust government and authorities increasingly less and, despite supporting democratic norms are disappointed with the supply of political goods—are searching for alternative avenues to make their voices heard. Only by studying *both* old and new forms of participation do we obtain a complete picture of the ways citizens are involved in politics. And only a complete picture like that will enable us to evaluate the quality of democracy systematically.

The voices of citizens using new forms of participation are mostly not captured by empirical research. This is quite paradoxical as one of the biggest concerns of participation research has been the perennial problem of participatory inequality and equal voice in the political arena (Schlozman, Verba, and Brady 2012). New forms of political participation might be part of the answer to that problem. As a result of this state of affairs, not only many of the appraisals of the state of democracy are dire, but solutions to the challenge of how to approach citizens and convince them that their voices count, remain under-informed.

We have argued that in order to capture political participation (and subsequently to draw conclusions about the quality of democracy), we should take new forms of participation seriously. This involves recognizing them, locating them, and only after doing that, trying to understand them. Understanding should involve investigating them not only from the researcher's side, aiming at citizens an array of pre-defined measures—frequently reflecting normative ideas of what scholars think participation ought to be—but also working the other way around by integrating into the study of participation citizens' own participatory understandings. Through the different chapters of this book, we have demonstrated the necessity for an approach *combining* the study of old and new forms of participation systematically, and have provided the conceptual and empirical tools for the implementation of such an integrated approach. It is our hope that these tools will stimulate interest in old and hard-to-detect new forms of participation in politics. Democracy certainly is worth these efforts.

References

Barnes, Samuel H, Max Kaase, Klaus R Allerbeck, Barbara G Farah, Felix Heunks, Ronald Inglehart, M Kent Jennings, Hans-Dieter Klingemann, Alan Marsh, and Leopold Rosenmayr. 1979. *Political Action: Mass Participation in Five Western Democracies*. Beverly Hills: Sage.

Bennett, Lance W. 2012. "The Personalization of Politics: Political Identity, Social Media, and Changing Patterns of Participation." *The ANNALS of the American Academy of Political and Social Science* 644 (1): 20–39.

Brandt, Patrick T, Benjamin E Bagozzi, Vito D'Orazio, Latifur Khan, and Yang Gao. 2017. "The Automated Discovery of Protest Stories from Text." *2017 Mershon Center for International Security Studies, Conference on Democracy, the State and Protest*. Columbus, Ohio.

Marsh, David, Therese O'Toole, and Su Jones. 2007. *Young People and Politics in the UK: Apathy or Alienaton?* London: Palgrave, Basingstoke.

Schlozman, Kay Lehman, Sidney Verba, and Henry E Brady. 2012. *The Unheavenly Chorus: Unequal Political Voice and the Broken Promise of American Democracy*. Princeton: Princeton University Press.

Wells, Chris. 2015. *The Civic Organization and the Digital Citizen*. Oxford: Oxford University Press.

Zuckerman, Ethan. 2014. "New Media, New Civics?" *Policy & Internet* 6 (2): 151–68.

Appendix
Questions on Political Participation

		yes	no
1	Did you vote in the last national election?	☐	☐

During the last twelve months, have you done any of the following:

		yes	no
2	Worked for a party or candidate	☐	☐
3	Contacted a politician or a state or government official about an issue or problem	☐	☐
4	Attended a meeting of a political party or other political organization	☐	☐
5	Donated money to a political party or other political organization	☐	☐
6	Worked for a political action group ("Bürgerinitiative" in Germany)	☐	☐
7	Signed a petition	☐	☐
8	Joined a demonstration	☐	☐
9	Donated money to a social, humanitarian or charitable organization	☐	☐
10	Volunteered in a social, humanitarian or charitable organization	☐	☐
11	Boycotted certain products for political or ethical reasons	☐	☐
12	Deliberately bought certain products for political or ethical reasons	☐	☐
13	Volunteered for a community project	☐	☐
14	Posted or shared links on social media (Facebook, Twitter, YouTube, etc) to political stories or articles for others to read	☐	☐
15	Commented on social media (Facebook, Twitter, YouTube, etc) on political or social issues	☐	☐
16	Encouraged other people to take action on a political or social issue using Facebook, Twitter or other social media platforms	☐	☐

yes   no

In Berlin a group of people planted flowers in abandoned sites without permission, in order to make their neighborhood more beautiful; In Vienna hundreds helped creating a miniature model of a city that could have been built instead of bailing out banks. In Ferguson, thousands shared photos on social media to protest the shooting of a young black man by a white policeman. Many other examples of such expressive actions can be thought of and these are only three examples.

17   During the last twelve months, have you been engaged in   ☐   ☐
any such actions to express your political or social views or
concerns?

18   If yes, what did you do?
(i) ....
(ii) ....
(iii) ....

Name Index

Subject Index